Moonshine Distiller's Training Manual

Christopher G. Yorke, M. Ed

Moonshine Distiller's Training Manual
By Christopher G. Yorke, M. Ed

Published by:
Mason Creek Publishing
2500 Sunrise Street
Kelso,WA 98626
(360)600-9615
cyorke57@gmail.com

Copyright © 2017, 2023 by Mason Creek Publishing

ISBN: 978-0-9986005-1-2
Printed in the United States of America
Library of Congress CIP Data Pending

Money Back Guarantee
If the Moonshine Distiller's Training Manual does not meet your expectations for any reason, return it to Mason Creek Publishing for a 100% refund. Book must be returned in good condition within 30 days of purchase date. Be sure to include your return address.

Contents

CHAPTER 3: How to Make Classic Moonshine 45

CHAPTER 4: Additional Moonshine Recipes

CHAPTER 5:
How to Create Your Own Moonshine Recipes

CHAPTER 6: Cleaning and Sanitizing Equipment

Distilling Safety

Expanded Glossary

Appendix Tables 146

From the Author 151

PREFACE

The purpose of the Moonshine Distiller's Training Manual is to "teach" you to make your own moonshine. Everything you need to know is in this manual. You won't need to read four different books or spend countless hours searching the internet for the information you need - it is ALL here. The book is contains the information and procedures you need to make moonshine and other spirits. It does not contain a bunch of useless information and pages of fluff like many distilling books do. There are many different approaches to distilling alcohol and making moonshine. This manual contains the basic concepts and the proven procedures you need in order to successfully make your own moonshine, including clear pictures of every step. I recommend that you read through chapters 1 and 2 first in order to get a good general overview of the moonshine making process and all of the supplies and equipment you will be using. Then, in the remaining chapters we will get into the detailed steps and procedures of cooking mash, fermentation, distilling, and bottling. Although the concepts covered in the book can be applied to the use of any kind of still, we will be illustrating the use of a copper alembic pot still. It is the oldest type of still, but still considered by many to produce the best, most flavorful moonshine. It is also a good type of still to use when learning the moonshine making process.

Please remember that in order to distill spirits legally you need a license. For a small distiller you can apply for a craft distiller's license. You will need to apply for a Federal license and check with the requirements of your particular State.

Chapter 1
Moonshine Basics

Moonshine is illegal whiskey made at home. Moonshine can be made of just about any organic material that can be fermented and distilled, but the most common type of moonshine is made of corn mash. It is not aged and has a high proof between 100 and 180. Back during the days of prohibition, between 1920 and 1933, the production and sale of liquor (spirits) was illegal in the United States. People would illegally distill spirits at night, in the "shine of the moon," to avoid being caught by the law. The term is thought to have originated in England. Early English whiskey smugglers were called "Moonrakers" because they worked by the light of the moon. You can find whiskey called Moonshine in liquor stores, but it is not actually moonshine. It is simply white dog (white whiskey) that has not been aged in an oak barrel and it (is) made legally. All distilled spirits start off as plain old ethanol, including moonshine. The various kinds of alcohol, including ethanol, come out of the still as clear as water.

The Process of Making Moonshine

This is a very short description of the moonshine-making process to get us started. First, a mixture of grain, or other organic biomass, is mixed with water and cooked to form a mash. The mash is cooled and yeast is added so that sugars in the mash can be converted into alcohol by the process of fermentation by yeast. The resulting fermented liquid (wash), which now contains alcohol, is heated in order to separate the various kinds of alcohol out of the wash (distillation). The distillate is separated out into foreshots, heads, hearts and tails. Then the hearts are bottled. Moonshine does not have to be aged. Again, this is a very short description. We will get deeper into the process as we proceed.

Basic Grain Science

Grain

Grain refers to the seed produced by plants in the grass family (gramineae). Most distilled spirits are made from grains including corn, barley, rye, wheat, oats and triticale. Traditional moonshine is made from corn, barley, and sugar. Although spirits in general, can be made from pretty much any kind of organic matter containing carbohydrates, the grains are the most popular.

Grain Anatomy

It is important to have a basic knowledge of grain anatomy in order to understand how alcohol is produced from fermented grains. Refer to the picture below as we discuss grain anatomy. This diagram shows a generic example of a grain (seed). It could be barley, rye, oats, or wheat. Although corn is also in the gramineae family, its structure is a little different that the other grains. The endosperm contains starch (carbohydrates). When water

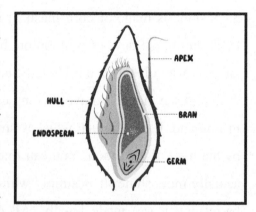

enters the seed, enzymes are activated that convert the starch to glucose (simple sugar). The embryo (germ), which is an immature plant, feeds on the glucose and water and begins to grow (germination). When we cook our mash we are allowing the natural enzymes in the grain, plus additional enzymes we add, to convert the starch into glucose. This is the process of saccharification. After the mash cools we add yeast which consumes the glucose (fermentation). As the yeast ferments the glucose it produces alcohol and carbon dioxide.

Corn

The scientific name for corn is Zea mays. There are 6 different types of corn in the Zea mays genus that are produced and used by humans, dent corn, flint corn, pod corn, popcorn, flour corn and sweet corn. Yellow dent corn (Zea mays var. indentata) is the primary corn used for ethanol and therefore whiskey production. Yellow dent corn has a high starch content compared to other varieties and that characteristic makes it good for making spirits.

Barley

The scientific name for barley is Hordeum vulgare. There are two main varieties, 2 row and 6 row. Two row barley has 2 rows of grain kernels on each head. It has a lower protein content, but higher carbohydrate (sugar) content. This is the primary kind used to make barley malt. Six row barley has 6 rows of grain kernels per head. It has more protein and a lower sugar content. It is primarily used as livestock feed.

Malted Barley

Malted barley, or barley malt, is made by soaking barley in water and initiating the germination (sprouting) process. The grain is then heated with hot air in order to stop germination. During this partial germination beta-amylase enzyme is produced inside the grain that helps convert starches in the grain into simple sugars like maltose and glucose. When malted barley is mixed with other grains in the mash the beta-amylase enzyme, plus alpha-amylase enzyme added by the distiller, converts all of the starches from all of the different grains in the mash into glucose. Malted grains, like malted barley, are often referred to as malt, referring to the maltose in the grain.

Oats

Oats, Avena sativa, are used to make bread, oatmeal, other baked goods and as livestock feed. There are a few distillers who make oat whiskey. The grain bill is usually 85% oats and 15% barley malt. Oats create a very smooth whiskey with a mellow, sweet, toasted grain flavor.

Rye

Rye is another cereal grain in the gramineae family. It's scientific name is Secale cereale. Rye is used to make flour, rye bread, rye beer, whiskey, vodka and is also used as livestock feed. Rye can be used to make rye whiskey, is part of the grain bill in bourbon, and is often used in making Canadian whiskey. It provides a spicy flavor to the whiskey. Early whiskey's in the United States were primarily made of rye since it was grown extensively at the time and was cheap. As the production of other grains like corn increased, other types of whiskey became more popular.

Wheat

Wheat, Triticum aestivum, is the second most produced grain in the world, topped only by corn. There are only a few straight wheat whiskeys produced in the world. However, there are many whiskeys which are "wheated," meaning that a small percentage of the grain bill includes wheat. Wheat tends to make whiskey smoother and sweeter tasting. The flavor profile of wheat whiskey is much milder than whiskey without wheat.

Grain Bill

In the distilling industry the grain bill is simply a list of which grains are used to make the mash and the percentage of each. For example, a common grain bill for Moonshine is 80% corn and 20% malted barley. Jack Daniels Tennessee Whiskey is 80% corn, 12% rye and 8% malted barley.

Mash

The mash consists of water, grains and enzymes added to help in the saccharification process. The mash is heated to specific temperatures and is rested for a certain length of time before adding yeast. The mashing process will be explained in greater detail later in the book.

Wort

The wort is the liquid produced from the mashing process. It contains glucose which will be fermented by yeast. By using a sugar hydrometer we can measure the specific gravity of the wort and determine what is known as the potential alcohol level.

Glucose, Maltose, Maltotriose

Glucose, maltose and maltotriose are the components of the starches found in the endosperm of cereal grains. Glucose ($C_6H_{12}O_6$) is the simplest sugar and is known as a monosaccharide meaning one glucose molecule. Maltose ($C_{12}H_{22}O_{11}$) is a disaccharide with two glucose molecules. Maltotriose ($C_{18}H_{32}O_{16}$) is a trisaccharide consisting of three glucose molecules. These sugars are present in the wort and are used by the yeasts during the process of fermentation.

Mashing

Mashing is the process of combining a mix of grains – typically malted barley, with other grains such as corn, rye, or wheat – known as the "mash bill," with water and then heating the mixture. The purpose of cooking a mash is to convert starches into fermentable sugars. The two main components of starch are Amylose and Amylopectin. They consist of thousands of glucose molecules linked together. These starches must be broken apart into individual glucose molecules to be fermentable by yeast. A mash is prepared by heating grain in water at the correct temperature, 63°C-66°C (145°F-151°F), adding enzymes, and allowing it to rest for 90 minutes. At these temperatures, the enzymes, called amylases, break down starches into simple sugars. Namely, glucose, sucrose, fructose, maltose, and maltotriose. Breaking down starch into sugars is a two-stage process. First, the starches are liquified through the process of **liquefaction.** During mash cooking alpha-amylase enzyme breaks the long starch chains into many smaller chains called dextrins. Immediately following liquefaction is the next process called **saccharification**, (aka conversion). During saccharification dextrins and other short chain starches are broken down by beta-amylase enzyme to glucose molecules that can be consumed by yeast during fermentation. Beta-amylase enzyme is plentiful in malted grains like malted barley. If you are making a mash without malted grains, and thus no beta-amylase, you can add an exogenous enzyme to do the job. Glucoamylase is a common enzyme to use in this situation.

pH (Potential of Hydrogen)

A pH reading measures the acidity and alkalinity of a substance. We are concerned about the pH of our mash during saccharification and our wort during to fermentation. The pH scale is a logarithmic scale that goes from 0 to 14. Seven is neutral, anything below 7 is acidic, and anything above 7 is alkaline. Acidic substances have a high concentration of hydrogen ions (H^+) and alkaline substances have a high concentration of hydroxyl ions (OH^-).

In the distilling business the optimum pH for mash is between 5.2 and 5.8, moderately acidic. This pH range improves the activity of the enzymes responsible for saccharification and gives us a better conversion of the starches in the mash to glucose. It is a good idea to check the pH of your mash with a pH test strip or a digital pH meter. The good news is that mash is naturally in the pH range of 5.2 to 5.8 because grains are acidic by nature.

The optimum pH for fermentation by the yeast is between 4.0-4.5. Yeast thrive in a acidic environment and are the most healthy in this pH range. This pH also helps control bacterial growth. You should check the pH of your wort prior to fermentation. If the pH values for either your mash of your wort are high or low you can adjust them quiet easily. For a pH that is too low, too acidic, you can add calcium carbonate (lime). Mix in 1/2 tsp at a time. Recheck your pH. Keep adding 1/2 tsp at a time until you get it into the correct range. For a pH that is to high, too alkaline, add citric acid or calcium sulfate (gypsum). Mix in 1/2 tsp at a time. Recheck your pH. Keep adding 1/2 tsp at a time until you get it into the correct range. When you check your pH levels you might find they are fine. However, there are variables that can cause your pH to be out of the correct range, one of which is your water.

Enzymes

Enzymes are very important proteins that act as **catalysts** (biocatalysts). Catalysts accelerate chemical reactions but are not consumed in the reactions. The molecules which enzymes act on are called substrates. The enzymes convert the substrates into different molecules known as products. During the mashing process enzymes are needed to help convert starches into fermentable sugars, this is known as **saccharification**. The required enzymes are provided by using malted barley in most cases. Malted barley, and other malted grains, provide four primary enzymes. They include alpha-amylase, beta-amylase, maltase, and limit dextrinase. These enzymes are produced by the grain (seed) during germination or sprouting. The enzymes **hydrolyze** the starches in the endosperm of the grain converting them into glucose that can be use as a food source by the newly germinating embryo. In the malting process utilized by commercial malting companies grains are moistened to allow germination to begin and then they are heated to stop germination. This process of "malting" preserves the enzymes so that we can use them for saccharification during the mashing process. A significant amount of maltose, a sugar containing 2 glucose molecules, is produced during malting, thus the name **malted grain**. The term **diastase** is used to refer to any one of the enzymes involved in converting starches into simpler sugars. The amount of enzymes present in a malted grain is known as the **diastatic power (DP)**. It is a measurement of the combined power of the enzymes needed to hydrolyze starch. The unit of measurement for DP is degrees **Lintner ($^{\circ}$L).** It refers to the combined starch degrading power (potential) for a pound of malted grain. One pound of a malted grain needs at least 30 $^{\circ}$L in order to convert the starches it contains into simple sugars like glucose. For a good conversion of starches to glucose during the mashing process, a DP of at least 40 $^{\circ}$L is recommended. It is easy to calculate the DP of a mash. Take the $^{\circ}$L for each grain, multiply by the pounds of each grain, add up the total $^{\circ}$L and divide by the total pounds of grain. The DP for some commonly used grains are listed in the table on page 8.

Example:

7 lbs. 2 Row Barley Malt, 7 X 150 = 1050

4 lbs. Rye (not malted), 6 X 0 = 0

13 lbs. Corn (not malted), 13 X 0 = 0

1050/24 lbs. total = 43.75 $^{\circ}$L

The DP is above 40 $^{\circ}$L so we are good to go.

If your DP is less than 40 you could add more barley malt or add a supplemental enzyme. Depending on what kind of moonshine you are making, you will need to select the correct enzymes to ensure a good conversion of starches to fermentable sugars (saccharification). On pages 35-36 we will look at various enzymes and their application in making moonshine. It is important to remember that enzymes work best in moderately hard water, at certain temperatures, and at certain pH levels. Be sure to adjust your water hardness if you have soft water, follow recommended mash cooking temperatures, and adjust you pH if needed. We will cover each of these procedures. It is best to adjust water hardness and pH before you add enzymes to your mash.

Hard Water

Hard water contains calcium and magnesium minerals. Enzymes need at least 50 ppm of calcium to do their job. If you have soft water you can add gypsum (calcium sulfate). One gram per gallon of water will result in about 61 ppm of calcium and also lowers the pH.

Gypsum: 1 teaspoon per 5 gallons of mash

Diastatic Power, Specific Gravity, and Potential Alcohol of Common Grains & Starches

GRAIN	DP °L	SPECIFIC GRAVITY	POTENTIAL ALCOHOL
Barley Malt, 2 row	140	1.036	4.7
Barley Malt, 6 row	160	1.035	4.6
Barley, flaked	0	1.032	4.2
Barley, peated	0	1.038	5.0
Barley, raw	0	1.028	3.7
Chocolate Barley Malt	0	1.034	4.5
Crystal Barley Malt	0	1.032	4.2
Corn, flaked	0	1.037	4.9
Corn Malt	20	1.037	4.9
Corn Meal	0	1.035	4.6
Oats	0	1.037	4.9
Oat Malt	25	1.037	4.9
Rice	0	1.032	4.2
Rye	0	1.036	4.7
Rye Malt	80	1.038	5.0
Wheat, white	0	1.030	3.9
Wheat, red	0	1.029	3.8
Wheat Malt, white	130	1.040	5.2
Wheat Malt, red	180	1.038	5.0

Yeast

Saccharomyces cerevisiae Pronounced (sa-kr-ow-mai-suhs seh-ruh-vi-see-ay), is the species of yeast used in making spirits. There are many strains within this species. Different strains produce a variety of esters during fermentation that affect the taste of the product being produced. Some preferred strains recommended for making moonshine and whiskey are listed below.

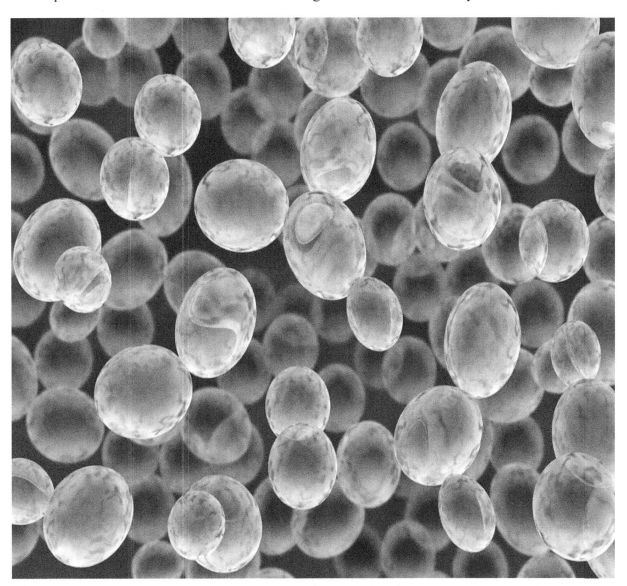

Fermentation

Fermentation is the process of converting sugars, like glucose and maltose, into acids, carbon dioxide (CO_2) and various alcohols by yeasts. Putting yeast into the mash or the wort, so they can consume glucose and produce alcohol, is called **pitching the yeast**. The alcohol we are primarily interested in is ethanol (C_2H_5OH). During both respiration and fermentation yeast cells break down glucose molecules to release energy. This is called **glycolysis.** The breakdown of glucose also releases carbon atoms which can be used by the yeast to grow and reproduce (budding). There are two primary methods of fermentation used in distilling alcohol, **fermenting on the grain** and **fermenting off the grain**. Mash bills that contain corn are usually fermented on the grain because corn is more difficult to sparge than all grain whiskeys. Moonshine, bourbon and Tennessee whiskeys are normally fermented on the grain, while single malt whiskeys, like Scotch whisky, and Irish whiskeys are normally fermented off the grain. Some believe that fermenting on the grain produces a more flavorful spirit.

Distillation

Distillation is the process of separating substances from a liquid mixture by heating, evaporating (forming a vapor), cooling and condensing vapor back into a liquid. Once the vapor is condensed back into a liquid it is referred to as the distillate. In the case of making moonshine the distillate is alcohol, primarily ethanol.

Aging Moonshine

Moonshine is not usually aged. However, you can age it if desired. Commercial distilleries use charred oak barrels to age their product. Barrels or casks made of American White Oak wood are the most commonly used structures for aging whiskey, although there are some variations to that. Oak barrels are expensive, large (53 gallon), and take years to properly age whiskey. An alternative to barrel aging is jar aging. This requires one-gallon glass jars with lids and either charred or toasted American White Oak cubes. The process is quite simple and will create excellent product in six months or less.

First off buy some one-gallon glass jars with lids. You can purchase oak cubes, but they are expensive. It is easy to get some white oak wood, cut it into small pieces and, either toast it in an oven or char it with a propane torch. You can char larger amounts by burning it on a camping stove. Put your newly distilled spirits into the jar, place a few oak chunks in, and label your jar. Your oak chucks should be about one-inch square. Jar aged whiskey starts to get good after a couple of months, but I recommend letting it age for at least 6 months.

Bottling Moonshine

If you don't age your moonshine you can bottle it immediately after distilling if you desire. You simply take your hearts and pour them into bottles. I prefer to place the hearts in a gallon jar, place three coffee filters over the top with a rubber band, and let it breath for a week before bottling. This allows volatile compounds to evaporate and improves the flavor. If you decide to age with charred or toasted wood, your moonshine will be ready to bottle when the color and taste are to your liking. It will normally take a minimum of two months for aging with wood. Of course, the longer you let it age the better it will be. I recommend six months for the best product. When the time arrives, get out your bottles, your funnel, some coffee filters, and filter your product into bottles. In my opinion, it is best not to filter moonshine through activated carbon or charcoal filters, they will strip out too many congeners and dilute the flavor of your moonshine. In the commercial distilling business they call it polishing. It might make the moonshine a little smoother, but it will reduce the flavor.

Chapter 2

Supplies and Equipment

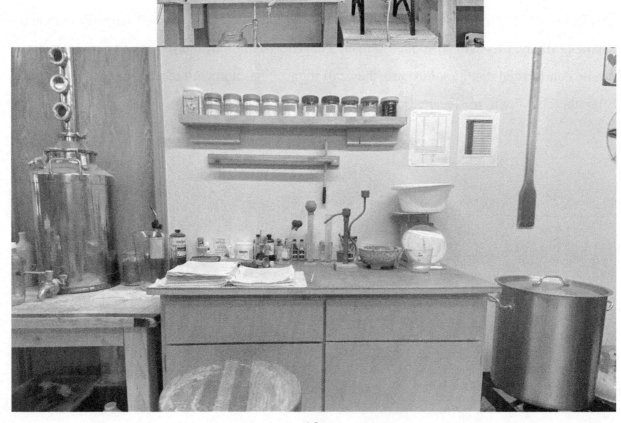

ALEMBIC POT STILL AND PARTS

The copper alembic pot still is the oldest type of still used. Many people, including some commercial distilleries, believe the Alembic Copper Still produces the best tasting spirits. It consists of the still, still head, vapor thermometer, condenser, coiled condenser tubing, (goes down into the condenser) and vapor thermometer. The wash is placed into the still and heated by the burner for distillation. Alcohol vapors accumulate in the still head, travel past the vapor thermometer and into the condenser tubing. As the vapor travels down the condenser tubing into the condenser, the cool water in the condenser converts the vapor back into liquid. The liquefied alcohol exits the condenser through the food-grade condenser discharge tube and goes into a distillate collection jar. Throughout this book we will be demonstrating the distilling process with the 8 gallon pot still shown below. This still was purchased from Mile High Distilling, it's a great still. If you have a different type of still, just follow the manufacturers instructions.

A - 8 gallon still

B - Still head

C - Vapor thermometer

D - Lyne Arm

E - Condenser

F - Food grade condenser discharge tube

G - Alcohol Parrot

H - Distillate collection jar   I - Propane Burner

CONDENSER PARTS AND SETUP

The condenser consists of a copper bucket with a coiled copper tube that brings the vaporized distillate from the still down through a supply of cool water. As the vapor enters the coiled copper tubing, which is in the cool water, the vapor returns to a liquid and drains out through the food grade tubing into your distillate collection jar.

A - Water line in, 1/2" black irrigation tubing, with 1/2" hose clamp.

    Brings water into condenser bucket.

B - Water line out, 1/2" black irrigation tubing, with 1/2" hose clamp.

    A long enough pipe to go outside to drain.

C - 1/2" food grade tubing connected with 1/2" hose clamp.

    For distillate outflow to collection jar.

CONDENSER COILED COPPER TUBING

Inside the condenser you find the coiled condenser tubing. During distillation the condenser is full of cool water that continuously flows into the condenser from an inflow line and leaves the condenser through an outflow line. This provides the cool water required to convert the alcohol vapors back into liquid form.

Inside of the condenser showing the coiled tubing.

ALCOHOL PARROT

The alcohol parrot is used to monitor the alcohol by volume (ABV) coming out of the still during distillation. This is very useful because you can watch the ABV continuously as you distill. The setup for the parrot is shown on the next page. You can purchase a parrot for about $50.

Alcohol Parrot

ALCOHOL PARROT AND COLLECTION JAR SETUP

The alcohol parrot collects distillate from the food grade distillate tube (A). The alcoholometer is placed into the parrot tube (B). Once the distillate has filled the parrot tube, ABV can be read off of the alcoholometer. See "how to use an alcoholometer" on page 19. Distillate flows out of the parrot and into the collection jar.

Alcohol Parrot Setup with distillate collection jar

ALCOHOLOMETER (ALCOHOL HYDROMETER)

The alcoholometer or alcohol hydrometer, measures the specific gravity of the distillate. Once you know the specific gravity you can determine the ABV. Specific gravity indicates how dense a liquid is. Alcohol is less dense than water so the hydrometer will sink lower in it compared to water. The picture below shows you how the hydrometer is placed into the alcohol parrot. See page 19 for a complete explanation of how the hydrometer works and how to use it. They are about $10.00 at Amazon.

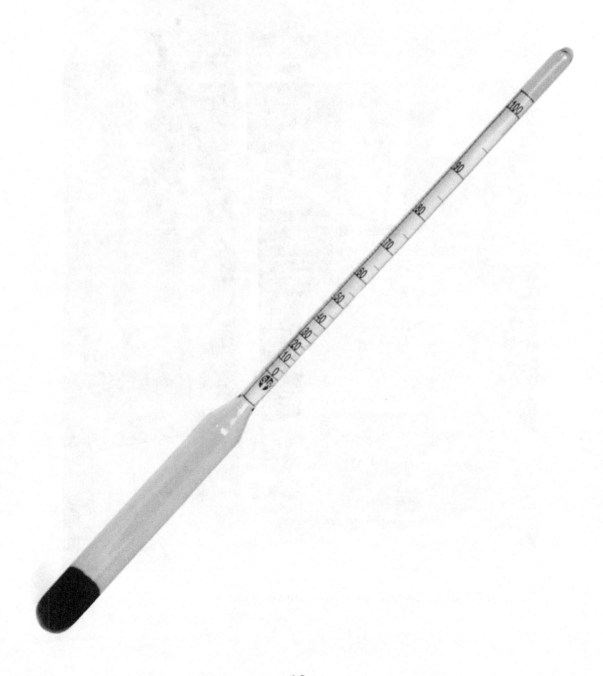

Alcoholometer (Alcohol hydrometer) - How to Use

The alcohol hydrometer has two scales, one on each side. One side shows the abv percentage and the other shows the proof. Proof is simply twice the abv. For example, 40% abv is 80 proof.

When you place the hydrometer into a parrot, graduated cylinder, or any other receptacle it will float and you can read the abv or proof. If your reading was as shown with the arrow on the next page, you would have an abv of 45% and a proof of 90.

Reading at the meniscus. This is very important. The meniscus is the curved upper surface of a liquid in a tube. When you place the hydrometer into the distillate a meniscus will form around it. Make sure you read at the bottom of the meniscus, not at the part that rises up on the side of the hydrometer. The picture below shows how to read the proof on an alcohol hydrometer correctly. In this case the correct reading would be 164 proof.

Each increment on the abv scale is 1.
Each increment on the proof scale is 2.

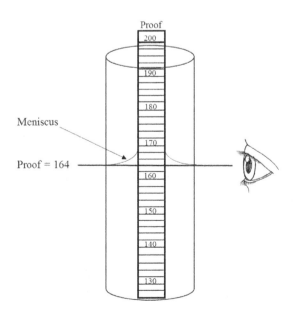

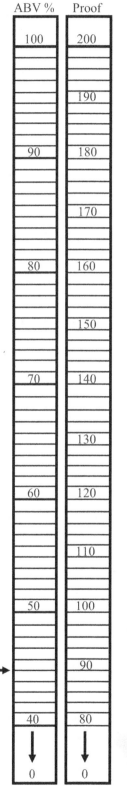

Adjusting abv for Temperatures
Above or Below 15.5°C (60°F)

The alcoholometer is calibrated to work at 15.5°C (60°F). If the temperature of your distillate is above or below 15.5°C (60°F) you need to make an adjustment to your reading. As the distillate temperature increases the alcohol becomes less dense, the hydrometer sinks lower into the distillate and you get a false high reading. You need to subtract from the hydrometer reading in order to get the correct abv. As the distillate temperature decreases the alcohol becomes more dense, the hydrometer rises and you get a false low reading. You need to add to the hydrometer reading in order to get the correct abv. The table on page 21 shows you the amounts to add or subtract at the various distillate temperatures. Make sure you check the <u>distillate temperature</u> and don't use the ambient air temperature when making these adjustments. Check the distillate temperature by inserting your long stem thermometer into your parrot tube.

(Photocopy the table and post it on the wall next to your still.)

ABV TEMPERATURE CORRECTION

Temp °F	0-25 Proof	25-50 Proof	50-200 Proof
100	-14	-12	-16
95	-12	-10.5	-14
90	-10	-9	-12
85	-8.5	-7.5	-10
80	-7	-6	-8
75	-5	-4.5	-6
70	-3	-3	-4
65	-1.5	-1.5	-2
60	0	0	0
55	+1.5	+1.5	+2
50	+3.5	+3	+4
45	+5	+4.5	+6
40	+7	+6	+8
35	+9	+8	+10
30	+10.5	+9	+12
25	+12	+10.5	+14
20	+14	+12	+16
15	+16	+13.5	+18
10	+18	+15	+20
5	+19	+16.5	+22
0	+21	+18	+24

Subtract from the abv reading when the distillate temperature is above 60°F.
Add to the abv reading when the distillate temperature is below 60°F.

21

SACCHAROMETER
(SUGAR HYDROMETER)

A saccharometer is a hydrometer used for determining the amount of sugar in a solution. In the case of making moonshine, the sugar hydrometer is used to measure the specific gravity (SG) in the mash, and the wash after fermentation is complete. Once we know the SG of the mash or the wash we can look at the potential alcohol side of the hydrometer to determine the predicted percentage of alcohol in the wort. We can also look at the table on page 23 to determine the potential alcohol for each corresponding specific gravity. Potential alcohol (PA) is an estimate of the percentage of the mash or wash that will become alcohol from fermentation by the yeast. It is important to recognize that the potential alcohol is an estimate of the total alcohol in the wort, not just the ethanol. The actual amount of ethanol, the alcohol we want, will be less than the total indicated by the PA reading. When you purchase a saccharometer a small version of the table on page 23 comes with it. A saccharometer can be purchased from a brew store or from Amazon.com for about $12.00.

READING THE SG AND PA

The more sugar that is in the mash or the wash the higher the SG will be. This means the density of the solution is higher. The higher the SG the higher the hydrometer will float in the solution. This will show a higher SG and PA reading on the hydrometer. As an example, look at the arrow on the right. The correct reading would be 1.070 for SG and 9.20 percent for PA. Again, using the table on page 23 will give you a more accurate reading.

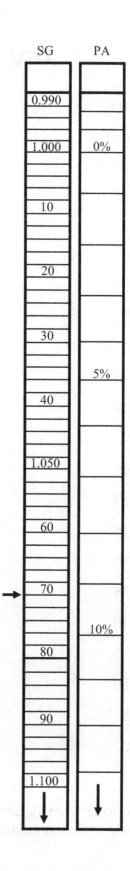

SPECIFIC GRAVITY & POTENTIAL ALCOHOL

Specific Gravity (20°C/68°F)	Potential Alcohol (%/Volume)
1.000	0.0
1.005	0.7
1.010	1.3
1.015	2.0
1.020	2.6
1.025	3.3
1.030	4.0
1.035	4.6
1.040	5.3
1.045	5.9
1.050	6.6
1.055	7.2
1.060	7.9
1.065	8.6
1.070	9.2
1.075	9.9
1.080	10.5
1.085	11.2
1.090	11.8
1.095	12.5
1.100	13.2
1.110	14.0

The saccharometer is calibrated to work at a temperature of 20°C (68°F). You need to know the temperature of your wort or your wash when taking a measurement. Use your long stem food thermometer to take the temperature. If the wort or wash is higher or lower the 20°C (68°F) use the following table to adjust your reading. Most saccharometers come with this table.

Temperature F°	Correction
54.2	- 0.002
61.5	- 0.001
68	-
73.7	+ 0.001
79.2	+ 0.002
84.3	+ 0.003

GRADUATED CYLINDER

The graduated cylinder is a necessary tool for using your hydrometers to measure specific gravity of your mash, wash and distillate. Remember that you are measuring the sugar content of your mash and wash in order to determine their potential alcohol. You are also measuring the abv of your distillate as you distill your wash. Fill the cylinder with fluid from your mash, your wash, or your still and place the appropriate hydrometer into the cylinder. A turkey baster works good for transferring fluid into the cylinder. Be sure to spin the hydrometer to eliminate any bubbles sticking to it. Just give it a slight spin, let it stop and take your reading. You can get a good graduated cylinder from a brew store or from Amazon.com for about $10.00.

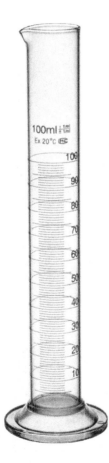

A graduated cylinder makes it easy to take your specific gravity measurements.

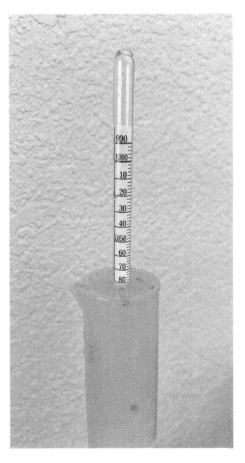

Using an alcohol hydrometer to measure abv in a graduated cylinder.

FIFTEEN GALLON COOKING POT WITH LID

The size of your cooking pot will depend on the size of your still and on how big of batches you plan to cook. I recommend a fifteen gallon, triple clad bottom pot. This will allow you to cook batches for a nine gallon (35 liter) still. Get a good quality pot with a triple clad bottom. The thick bottom of a pot like this will help prevent burning your mash on the bottom. A good quality cooking pot can be purchased at a brew store for about $85.00.

LARGE MASH PADDLE

A nice large mash paddle makes mash cooking much easier. You can also use large stirring spoons, but if you do, stirring your mash will be a lot more work. You can find a wooden paddle like the one pictured on Amazon.com for $15.00.

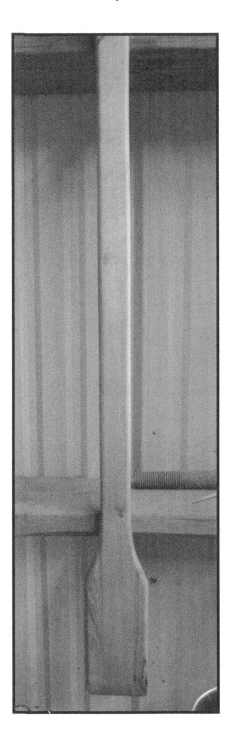

FOOD GRADE LONG STEM THERMOMETER

Used to check temperature of mash and distillate. Long stem thermometers are available at brew stores and Amazon.com for $10.00.

PROPANE BURNER FOR COOKING MASH
5 GALLON PROPANE TANK

The Bayou Country Classic propane burner is perfect for cooking large batches of mash. These are available at stores like Walmart, Lowe's, brew stores and like everything, at Amazon.com. They cost about $60.00. Propane tanks are available everywhere. They cost about $45.00.

ELECTRIC HOT PLATE BURNER

You need an electric burner with at least 1500 watts for distilling. If you get one that is less than 1500 watts it will take forever to heat your wash when distilling. A decent burner will cost around $50.00. They are available at most department stores and Amazon.com. Some people use propane burners for distilling. Extra precautions are needed if using an open flame .

EIGHT OUNCE CANNING JARS

You will need around twenty four 8 ounce canning jars. These will be used during the spirit run. The spirit run is the second distillation you will do on each batch. It is the run where you will be collecting the final product and dividing it into four ounce increments as you distill. This process will be explained in full detail in the distillation chapter. You can get canning jars at any department store for about $8.00 for a case of twelve.

ONE GALLON STORAGE JARS

Gallon jars can be used to store and/or aging your moonshine. I recommend buying four or five of them to start with. You can get them at brew stores for $7.00.

AGING JAR LABELS

It is really important to accurately label your aging jars or things will get mixed up and you won't know what you have in each jar. Photocopy the labels on page 31 and use them for labeling your jars.

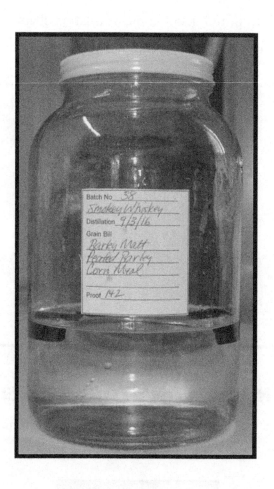

AGING JAR LABELS

Batch No_____

_____

Distillation_____

Grain Bill

_____

_____

_____

_____

Proof_____

Batch No_____

_____

Distillation_____

Grain Bill

_____

_____

_____

_____

Proof_____

Batch No_____

_____

Distillation_____

Grain Bill

_____

_____

_____

_____

Proof_____

Batch No_____

_____

Distillation_____

Grain Bill

_____

_____

_____

_____

Proof_____

Distillation: Date of spirit run.
Grain Bill: Each grain and percentage.

FERMENTATION ROOM

A room dedicated to fermentation is a nice feature of a distillery. In this room you will ferment your batches of mash and extract the fermented wash when fermentation is complete. The process can be messy at times, so a tile or concrete floor is best. Controlling ambient temperature is also much easier in a dedicated room. A trailer winch is mounted to a beam and used to pull the mash bag from the fermenter when fermentation is complete.

YEAST

There are many types of yeast available on the market. The list here includes some good yeast products that work well for making moonshine.

Distiller's Whiskey Yeast, Still Spirits

American Whiskey Yeast, Safspirit

High Spirits Whiskey Yeast, High Spirits

Whiskey Pure Yeast, Liquor Quik

DistilaMax MW Grain Whiskey Yeast, Lallemand

Light Whiskey Yeast, White Star

Distiller's Active Dry Yeast (DADY)

Bread Yeast

Malt Whiskey Yeast, Safspirit

DistilaMax MW Grain Whiskey Yeast works great for making moonshine.

YEAST NUTRIENTS

Yeast must have an adequate supply of nutrients for successful growth and fermentation. They need a source of nitrogen in order to synthesize proteins. They also need the B vitamins biotin, thiamin, and pantothenic acid. And they need the minerals magnesium and zinc. Some of these nutrients will be supplied by the grains or other items in your grain bill, but it is always a good practice to include a well balanced nutrient supplement to ensure healthy yeast growth and reproduction. There are many yeast nutrient products available on the market and I have used many of them over the years.

FERMAX

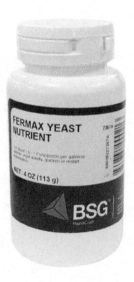

My favorite is **Fermax** yeast nutrient. It contains diammonium phosphate (DAP), magnesium sulfate, yeast hulls, B vitamins and calcium salts, it supplies all important nutrients that yeast require for a healthy fermentation. You can also use it to restart a stuck fermentation. Available at brew stores and online.

Rate: 1 teaspoon per gallon of mash or wash

When to Add: Add Fermax prior to pitching your yeast, mix in well

DIAMONNIUM PHOSPHATE (DAP)

DAP is a good source of nitrogen and will help keep the yeast active during fermentation. It is recommended for juice washes and high sugar washes that do not contain grain. Some nutrient blends contain DAP so you don't need to add anymore if using those. High sugar washes for some moonshine recipes may benefit from the addition of DAP. It is added prior to fermentation at the same time yeast is pitched. Mash composed of mostly grain will contain enough nitrogen to make the addition of DAP unnecessary.

Rate: 1/2 teaspoon per 5 gallons of mash or wash

When to Add: Add DAP prior to pitching your yeast, mix in well

ALPHA-AMYLASE ENZYME

Alpha amylase enzyme is released from the aleurone layer that surrounds the endosperm of a grain (seed) like barley. The endosperm of the grain contains the starches which are a source of energy for the germinating embryo. The enzyme hydrolyzes and breaks chemical bonds in starch molecules, which are long chains of glucose molecules, into many smaller chains. The smaller chains are then exposed to further digestion by beta amylase enzyme. Many distillers add commercial alpha amylase enzyme to their mashes just to make sure there's an adequate amount. I recommend using this enzyme in all of your vodka mashes. It is available at brew stores and at Amazon.com.

Alpha-amylase Rate: ½ tsp per 5 gallons of mash
Optimum Temperature Range: 65-72°C (149-162°F)
Optimum pH: 5.3-5.7

BETA-AMYLASE ENZYME

Beta amylase enzyme is produced in the endosperm of grains during germination. The enzyme can degrade and break apart amylose (a type of starch) and dextrins. It breaks the second chemical bond in a starch molecule and produces molecules of maltose. Maltose is composed of 2 glucose molecules. Malted grain posses enough beta-amylase to convert its own starches into simple sugars, like glucose, and enough to convert the starches in the other grains in a mash as well. Malted grains that provide diastatic power to the grain bill are called **base malts**.

Rate: Adequate supply in malted grains.
Optimum Temperature Range: 55-66°C (131-150°F)
Optimum pH: 5.1-5.3

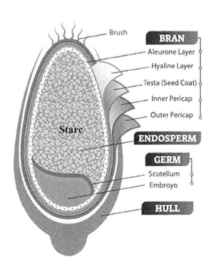

GLUCOAMYLASE ENZYME

Glucoamylase is a **exogenous** enzyme that hydrolyzes short chain dextrins into fermentable sugars. Exogenous means the enzyme is not found in malted grains; it is added from a source outside the grain. It is not needed unless you are preparing a mash of raw grains (not malted) or other starch based substrates like potatoes. If you are preparing a mash with barley malt included, you do not need glucoamylase. It can be purchased at brew stores or online if needed.

Allow the mash to cool to 60°C (140°F) before adding the glucoamylase enzyme. Glucoamylase enzyme is deactivated at temperatures above 60°C (149°F). It works best in a temperature range of 50-60°C (122-140°F), but will remain active between 30-65°C (86-149°F). So it will actually be converting some starches (like dextrins) during the first part of fermentation.

Rate: 1/2 teaspoon per 5 gallons mash

Optimum Temperature Range: 55-60°C (131-140°F)

Optimum pH: 2.8-5.0

PECTIC ENZYME

Pectic enzyme is used to help break down the pectin in fruit pomace and juice and release more fermentable sugars for the yeast to consume. Use when making fruit moonshine. Not needed for grain mash or sugar based washes. Add pectic enzyme to a fruit mash when the mash has cooled and just prior to fermentation.

Rate: 1/2 teaspoon per gallon of mash

Optimum Temperature Range: 18-40°C (64-104°F)

Optimum pH: 4.5-5.5

pH METER

A good digital pH meter is the best way to go. Test strips are not very accurate. You will need a pH meter to check the pH of mash during saccharification and during fermentation. One like this runs about $90.

12 GALLON FERMENTER WITH LID

A 12 gallon fermenter is just the right size to use for an 8 gallon still. To use an 8 gallon still you should plan to cook your batches with 8 gallons of water and 24 pounds of grain yielding about a 10 gallon mash. After fermentation you will end up with about 6 gallons of wash. This will fit perfectly into an 8 gallon still. You shouldn't fill your still much more than about 3/4 full of wash for distilling. Note: You do not need to use a carboy and pressure valve to ferment your wort. We will discuss this in detail in the fermentation chapter. You can buy a 12 gallon fermenter for about $40.00 at brew stores.

12 Gallon Fermenter
with Lid

MASH BAG

The mash bag is placed inside your fermenting bucket. After you have cooked your mash, it has cooled to about 24ºC (75ºF), you have pitched the yeast, mixed it well, and aerated the mash, you pour the mash into the bag. This makes it easy to remove the mash from the fermenting bucket once fermentation is complete. This will be covered in detail in the fermentation chapter. These cost $7.00 at brew stores.

Mash poured into the mash bag which is in the fermentation bucket.

Mash Bag

FOOD SCALE

A good food scale is necessary for weighing your grain. You can get one at most department stores for about $40.00.

PLASTIC BOWL

A basic plastic salad or mixing bowl works well for measuring and weighing your grain, transferring grain into your cooking pot, transferring mash into your fermentation bucket and for transferring your wash into your still.

FLOUR FOR SEALING STILL HEAD

You will need to make a flour paste for sealing your still head. The head is removeable and must be sealed when distilling to prevent vapor loss. Mix 1 Tbs of flour with about 1 Tbs of water and mix it together. You should end up with a thick paste similar to pancake batter. Spread it around your still head seam with your finger and you are good to go.

Sealing the still head with flour paste.

40

KITCHEN STRAINER

A kitchen strainer is useful for taking samples of your wort when checking specific gravity. Place it into the mash pot to separate the wort from the grains.

TURKEY BASTER

Use a turkey baster to draw samples from your wort and your wash. The picture on the left below shows how to draw a sample of wort from the mash pot. The picture on the right shows drawing a sample from your fermentation bucket. Just place the turkey baster down in between the mash bag and the bucket. Draw it out and place it into you graduated cylinder, put your saccharometer in and read your SG.

DUCT TAPE

You will need duct tape for recording your temperature and abv as you distill using the 24 pint sized canning jars. Place a line of duct tape on the edge of a table as shown below. As you fill your small jars half full during distillation, you will place them on the table and record the vapor temperature and abv. This example shows the temperature in Celsius. Some stills have a Celsius vapor thermometer and some have Fahrenheit. You will be reading the abv from the alcohol hydrometer placed in your parrot.

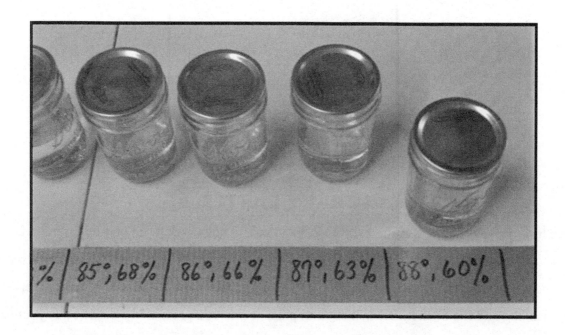

You will also need to record the batch number and date on your fermenter lid. Duct tape works well for that also.

MISCELLANEOUS SUPPLIES

16 Ounce Measuring Cup

Works well for measuring the quantity of distillate.

Purified Water

Use for proofing down you moonshine if desired.

Plastic Funnel

Use to pour moonshine into bottles.

Coffee Filters

Great for filtering spirits when pouring from aging jars into bottles. Also used to cover aging jars during the first 2 weeks of aging.

Storage Tub with Lid

A plastic tub works great for storing your supplies like hydrometers and other small items.

Shop Rags

Shop rags will be used throughout the moonshine making process.

Sharpies

Use a sharpie to record your temperature and abv when distilling and for labeling your fermenters when fermenting.

Duct Tape

Place a line of duct tape on your table to record abv and temperature when distilling.

Rubber Bands

For attaching coffee filters to the top of your aging jars.

Scrubber Pads and/or Scrubbing Brush

Scrubber pads or a scrubber brush will work well for cleaning your still and other equipment.

Cleaning Station, Hose

An outdoor wood bench, hose, and running water are nice to have for cleaning and rinsing your equipment.

Bleach

Use for cleaning and sanitizing non-copper equipment.

Space Heather with Thermostat

A small space heater with a thermostat makes it easy to control the temperature in your fermentation chamber.

Five Gallon Buckets with Handles

You will need two 5 gallon buckets for aerating your mash and transferring your fermented wash into your still.

Garbage Can with Lid

Needed for grain storage.

White Vinegar

Used for cleaning copper equipment.

Chapter 3
How to Make
Classic Moonshine

Y ou've read the first two chapters and you have all the necessary supplies and equipment - it's time to make moonshine!

For our example we will choose a classic moonshine grain bill and we'll use that example to show you each step in the moonshine making process. Everything we do will be calculated for an 8 gallon still. I recommend this size. It is easy to work with and will produce three to four fifths of final product per batch. If you have a different sized still it is easy to modify the grain bill based on the 8 gallon still quantities.

At the end of this chapter there is a Moonshine Worksheet that can be used as a guide and record when making this batch. If you actually make this recipe it will help you stay on track and provide a good place to record data. I recommend photocopying these worksheets and using them when you are making your spirits. Record keeping is extremely important! It will help you keep track of what works and what doesn't work. Record keeping will also make is easy to reproduce batches of spirits that you really like.

AMOUNT OF GRAIN TO USE

Moonshine grain bills normally have from 2 to 3 lbs. of grain per gallon of water. I recommend using 3 lbs. of grain per gallon of water. A good target range for original gravity is 1.065 to 1.095. This would be a potential alcohol range of 8.6% to 12.5%. This is a range that will produce an adequate amount of final product and will not create a problem for your yeast. Too high a sugar concentration in the wort or the wash can stress or even kill off the yeast. The same problem can occur if the alcohol concentration in the fermenting wort or the wash is too high. Most yeast strains can tolerate an alcohol concentration of 10 - 15%. I would stay well below 15% unless you are using a yeast strain with a high alcohol tolerance. For our example batch we will use 8 gallons of water and 24 lbs. of grain, (3 X 8 = 24 lbs. of grain). This will produce about 10 gallons of mash due to the added volume of the grain. Follow the cooking instructions in chapter 4 carefully! The amount of actual wash going into the still after fermentation will be about 6 gallons, just right for an 8 gallon still. You shouldn't fill your still much more than about three fourths full.

CLASSIC CORN MOONSHINE

We will use this recipe for our moonshine production example in chapter's 4-12. The still used is an 8 gallon copper alembic pot still. Read through this example batch to gain an understanding of the entire process. It would be even better if you were to actually produce this batch and learn from the process.

Recipe
Water - 8 gallons (10 gallons total mash volume - explained on page 47)
Corn Meal - 85%, 20.4 lb. (.85 X 24)
Barely Malt - 15%, 3.6 lb. (.15 X 24)
1 Teaspoon Amylase Enzyme (1/2 teaspoon per 5 gallons mash)
10 Teaspoons Fermax Yeast Nutrient (1 teaspoon per gallon mash)
5 Teaspoons Yeast, (1/2 teaspoon per gallon mash)

Note: If you use a different yeast nutrient just follow the directions on the package.

This grain bill should produce an expected original gravity of about 1.066 and an expected potential alcohol of about 8.7%.

HOW TO CALCULATE THE TOTAL WATER NEEDED

8 Gallon Still Example

To determine the amount of water needed for your mash, use the volume of your still. For an 8 gallon still we would use 8 gallons of water. This seems like it would be too much, but it works out at the end.

HOW TO CALCULATE THE TOTAL MASH VOLUME

The actual volume of mash will come out to be more than the amount of water you use. This is because the grains, and sugar if called for, will add some volume to the total mash quantity. You can estimate the added volume from the grain by multiplying **.08** times the number of pounds of grain and adding it to the gallons of water. .08 is the estimated amount, in gallons, that one pound of grain will add to the total mash volume. The reason the grain adds only a fractional amount to the total mash volume is due to the porosity of the grain particles, or the air space between the particles. This space fills with water. The grain also absorbs some of the water as well.

8 gal. water X 3 lbs. grain = 24 lbs. grain needed

24 X .08 = 1.92 gal. added volume from grain (round off to 2 gal.)

8 + 2 = 10 gal. total mash volume

The question is, will the wash from this batch fit into your still? Remember, you don't want to fill your still more the 3/4 full. You will typically get about 60% of your total mash volume returned as wash.

10 gal. mash X .60 (percentage of wash recovered from mash) = 6.0 gal. wash

6/8 = .75

This wash will fill 75% of your still. The 10 gallon mash will work.

The math calculations can help you meet the volume limits of your still. You don't need to meet those figures exactly. They are just guidelines. When cooking batches for your own still you will need to experiment and make adjustments as necessary.

BASIC STRUCTURE OF MOONSHINE RECIPES

Water - Better quality water makes better quality moonshine.

Grain Bill - Corn, Barley, etc.

Alpha-amylase enzyme - 1/2 tsp per 5 gallons of mash

Glucoamylase enzyme - 1/2 tsp per 5 gal. mash

   (not needed if using malted grains with diastatic power of at least 40°L)

Fermax yeast nutrient - 1 tsp per gallon of mash

Yeast - 1/2 tsp per gallon of mash

HOW TO CALCULATE GRAIN QUANTITIES

CLASSIC CORN MOONSHINE

Corn Meal - 85%

Barley Malt - 15% (needed to supply enzymes to the mash)

Alpha-amylase Enzyme - 1/2 teaspoon per 5 gallons mash

Fermax Yeast Nutrient - 1 teaspoon per gallons mash

Yeast - 1/2 teaspoon per gallon mash

Example for 8 gallon still

8 Gallons of water

24 Pounds of grain (8 gal. water X 3 lbs. grain = 24 lbs. grain needed)

10 Gallon mash

Just multiply the percentage of each kind of grain in your grain bill by the total amount of grain required.

Corn Meal - .85 X 24 lbs. grain = 20.4 lbs. Corm Meal

Barley Malt - .15 X 24 lbs. grain = 3.6 lbs. Barley Malt (Adds enzymes to the mash)

Alpha-amylase Enzyme - 1t (1/2 teaspoon per 5 gallons mash)

Fermax Yeast Nutrient - 10 t (1 teaspoon per gallon mash)

Yeast - 5 t (1/2 teaspoon per gallon mash)

Note: Remember that the grain quantities are based on the amount of water you are making your mash with. The water quantity is determined by the size of your still. See page 47. The goal is to make the largest batch possible in order to maximize production of moonshine.

Cooking the Mash for Classic Moonshine

WE WILL USE THE EXAMPLE MOONSHINE GRAIN BILL AND RECIPE FROM PAGE 46. YOU CAN USE THE FOLLOWING PROCESS FOR MOONSHINE AND ANY GRAIN BASED SPIRIT RECIPE.

STEPS FOR COOKING THE MASH

1. PUT 8 GALLONS OF WATER INTO YOUR COOKING POT

2. HEAT THE WATER TO 75ºC (167ºF).

3. ADD THE CORN MEAL AND GELATINIZE FOR 1 HOUR

For any grain bill that includes corn, the corn must be gelatinized. Put in 20.4 lbs. of corn meal. Stir constantly as you add the corn or you will get corn dough balls that are hard to mix in. Once it is well mixed, put the lid on the pot and let it sit for one hour. You want to keep the temperature between 70ºC (158ºF) and 75ºC (167ºF). The corn mash will get very thick. It will liquefy after you mix in the alpha-amylase enzyme later on.

Mix the corn in thoroughly.

Put the lid on and let rest for one hour.

4. ALLOW THE TEMPERATURE TO DROP TO 64°C (148°F)

5. ADD THE ALPHA-AMYLASE ENZYME

Mix in the enzyme. This will liquify the gelatinized corn.

6. ADD THE BARLEY MALT

Allow the mash temperature to drop to 64°C (148°F) then mix in the barley malt. Add heat to keep the temperature at 64°C (148°F).

7. CHECK THE MASH pH

Take a sample of wort, allow it to drop to room temperature, and check the pH. You want between 5.2 and 5.8. Adjust as necessary.

8. REST THE MASH FOR 90 MINUTES AT 64°C (148°F)

Put the lid on the pot and allow to rest. Saccharification is occurring in this step. Keep temperature at 64°C (148°F). If ambient temperature is cold, wrap the pot with a blanket.

9. COOL THE MASH TO 24-27°C (75-80°F)

Use a wort chiller or let it rest overnight.

10. CHECK THE SPECIFIC GRAVITY OF THE WORT

Once the wort has cooled to between 24-27ºC (75-80ºF), place your kitchen strainer into the mash bucket to separate some wort from the grain. Using your turkey baster draw some wort and place it into your graduated cylinder. Fill it to within about 3 inches of the top. Use your saccharometer to check the specific gravity of the wort. It should read somewhere around 1.080 which equates to a potential alcohol of 10.5%. Your actual SG could be a little less or a little more. This will be your original gravity (OG). Your potential alcohol (PA) should be between 8 and 11%. Every batch will vary by a small amount. Not to worry. Record your OG and PA in your distillation worksheet (record).

Drawing out some wort using a kitchen strainer and turkey baster.

Placing the wort into the graduated cylinder.

Placing the saccharometer into the graduated cylinder
and reading the SG.

Fermentation

1. SANITIZE YOUR EQUIPMENT

Pour about 1 tablespoon of bleach into one of your 5 gallon buckets. Add a couple of gallons of water. Use that to wash out your other 5 gallon bucket, your mash bag, your plastic salad bowl and your fermentation bucket and lid. Rinse off everything with running water. I recommend doing this outside of your building with a hose. Use the triple rinse method. That is, rinse everything off or out three times. See chapter 15 for more information on sanitizing equipment.

2. PLACE YOUR MASH BAG INTO THE FERMENTER AND TIE IT IN PLACE

3. CHECK TO MAKE SURE YOUR MASH TEMPERATURE IS BETWEEN 24-27°C (75-80°F)

4. CHECK THE MASH pH

pH should be between 4.0-4.5. Adjust as necessary

5. ADD YEAST NUTRIENTS

Mix the nutrients in well.

6. PITCH THE YEAST

You will use 1/2 teaspoon of yeast per gallon of mash.

Get your yeast from the refrigerator, place 5 teaspoons in a small plastic bag or bowl and let it warm to room temperature for about 15 minutes. You don't want to pitch cold yeast into a batch of warm wort, the quick temperature change could kill the yeast. Mix the yeast in well.

7. AERATE THE MASH

Remove the mash using your plastic bowl. It is much easier to do it with a bowl in small amounts rather than trying to lift and pour your whole cooking pot. Pour bowls of mash into a 5 gallon bucket until the bucket is about half full. Next pour the mash between your two five gallon buckets three times. This will aerate the mash. After aerating, pour the half bucket into your fermenter. Keep doing this until the mash pot is empty and all of the mash is in your fermenter.

Pouring mash from the cooking pot into a 5 gallon bucket.

Aerating the mash by pouring between two buckets three times.

8. POUR THE MASH INTO YOUR FERMENTER

9. PUT THE LID ON YOUR FERMENTER AND LABEL IT

Include the batch number, date, time, and original gravity

10. PUT THE FERMENTER INTO YOUR FERMENTATION ROOM

11. SET YOU HEATER BETWEEN 24 AND 27°C (75-80°F)

Pouring mash into the fermenter.

Procedures During Fermentation

1. CHECK FOR THE GRAIN CAP AND CRACKLING SOUND

Check your batch after the first 2 to 3 hours. Pull the lid off of the fermenting bucket. You should see the grain cap. When the yeast really start growing and producing CO_2, a grain cap will form at the top of the fermentation bucket. This is a good sign because it shows that the yeast are actively fermenting. You should also be able to hear a distinct crackling sound, like Rice Krispies in a bowl of milk. That is the sound of the CO_2 bubbling up to the surface.

The grain cap can vary from really thick to quite thin depending on the particular grain bill you are using.

2. CHECK THE TEMPERATURE OF THE FERMENTATION ROOM
Keep the temperature around 24-27°C (75-80°F).

3. CHECK THE SG OF THE WASH

Check the SG every couple of days and record the data in your moonshine worksheet. The SG should be close to 1.000 when fermentation is complete. Fermentation should be complete in 3 to 5 days. When your SG is at 1.000 or close to it, all or most of the glucose has been converted to alcohol and the yeast are dying off. You will not the hear the crackling sound any longer and the grain cap may have sunk back into the wash. Fermentation is complete at this point. It's time to pull the mash bag and recover the wash. To calculate your Net PA subtract the ending PA from the beginning PA.

Remove the lid off of your fermenter. Pull the mash bag in a few inches in order to separate the wash from the grain. Draw wash out using your turkey baster and fill your graduated cylinder up to about 3 inches from the top.

Filling the graduated cylinder with wash.

Recovering the Wash

The wort, which was the liquid with the mash, has been fermented and is now called the wash. It will normally contain between 8 and 10% alcohol. Our task now is to separate the wash from the mash and prepare for distillation.

1. OPEN THE FERMENTER AND TIE A ROPE AROUND THE TOP OF THE MASH BAG

2. PULL THE MASH BAG OUT OF THE FERMENTER

You can pull the mash bag out by hand if you have a really strong back. Otherwise, I like the trailer winch method. Mount a trailer winch to a beam above your fermenter. Tie a rope around the top of the mash bag and tie a loop at the end of the rope. Put the loop onto the trailer winch hook and crank it up - really easy.

Pulling the mash bag out of the fermenter with a trailer winch.

3. ALLOW THE MASH BAG TO DRAIN

I recommend allowing the mash bag to drain back into the fermenter for several hours. You can also let it drain overnight if desired.

4. PRESS OUT THE REMAINING WASH

There are many ways to squeeze out the last bit of wash, you can't get it all with your hands. You could use a home-made mash press like the one shown below or you can create your own method. For a 10 gallon mash you should end up with 6 to 6½ gallons of wash.

5. ALLOW THE WASH TO SETTLE FOR TWO DAYS

Place the lid back on the fermenter and let the wash settle. After it settles you will see about an inch layer of material settled in the bottom, this is called trub (troob). It consists of fats, proteins, dormant and dead yeast. The yeast that has also settled with the trub is called the lees.

Home-Made Mash Press

If you want to save some money you can easily make a mash press from some basic materials that will work great. The one pictured uses a **livestock water tub**, a **plastic milk jug crate**, and a **block of wood**. Put the crate on top of the tub, place the mash bag into the crate, place the block of wood on top of the mash bag, and stand on it. Your weight will press out more of the wort. Be sure to have something to hold onto when you stand on the block of wood so you don't fall.

First Distillation
Stripping Run

Now the fun part begins, seeing your product start to flow. The stripping run has the sole purpose of getting all of the alcohol out of the wash. That includes the good stuff and the not so good stuff. Follow the steps outlined in this chapter and your stripping run will be a success.

1. REMOVE THE WASH FROM THE FERMENTER

Remove the mash bag from your fermenter. Next, begin ladling out the wash into a five gallon bucket with your plastic bowl. You could also use an auto-siphon for this process. Fill the bucket about half way with wash. Pour the wash from the bucket into your still. Keep doing this until all of the wash is in the still. Be sure to leave the trub in the bottom of the fermenter.

Removing the wash from the fermentation bucket.

2. POUR THE WASH INTO THE STILL

Each time you collect about half a bucket of wash pour it into your still. If your fermenter is located close enough you could just ladle the wash directly into the still. Otherwise, moving the wash to the still with a 5 gallon bucket works very well.

3. ATTACH THE HEAD ONTO THE STILL AND FASTEN THE CONDENSER TUBE

Place the still head on top of the still. Fasten the still head tube to the condenser tube. If your still has a fastening nut for connecting the head tube to the condenser tube, tighten it by hand, doesn't need to be too tight. Using the side of your hand, lightly pound the still head into place on the still. You want the still head to sit squarely onto the still with the seam even all the way around.

Pouring the wash into the still.

Lightly pounding the still head in place.

Fastening the lyne arm to the condenser tube.

4. SEAL THE STILL HEAD

Make up some flour paste and seal your still head.

Sealing the still head with flour paste.

5. SET UP 1 GALLON COLLECTION JAR AND ALCOHOL PARROT

For the stripping run you will use a 1 gallon jar to collect the distillate. Place the jar on a small table or small wooden box so it sits below you condenser. Place the food grade condenser collection tube into the top of your parrot. Position the parrot tube so that distillate will flow into your gallon jar from the parrot. Place your alcohol hydrometer inside the parrot as shown.

Correct still setup. Food grade tube from the condenser goes into the top of the alcohol parrot. The alcohol hydrometer is correctly placed into the parrot. The parrot is positioned to allow distillate to flow into the 1 gallon collection jar.

This picture shows the food grade condenser tube feeding into the top of the parrot, the correct placement of the alcohol hydrometer and the correct positioning of the parrot so that distillate will flow into the collection jar.

6. TURN ON YOUR BURNER

The goal is to heat up the wash slowly. Start with medium heat. If you heat it up too fast you could burn the wash and you could vaporize the liquid too fast. This would result in too high a concentration of water coming through with your alcohol. So go slow! As the run progresses you will need to increase the temperature a little at a time. You may need to decrease the temperature at certain points as well. You will know it is time to increase the temperature when the distillate dripping rate slows way down. It will take a couple of hours before you see any distillate dripping from your collection tube. Then things will speed up.

7. TURN ON THE CONDENSER WATER LINE

Turn on your water line to the condenser immediately before or after turning on your burner. Just a trickle will do. The water will slowly come in through the bottom waterline and will slowly trickle out of the top outlet line. This will keep your condenser water cool enough to liquefy the vapor coming from the still. You must make sure the incoming water is cold. Also make

sure your outflow line is set up to drain outside or into some kind of drain.

8. COLLECT THE DISTILLATE, MONITOR TEMP., MONITOR ABV

You should see your first drips of distillate after about 3 hours. The vapor temperature will be around 60°C (140°F). When your parrot fills with distillate you will be able to start observing the abv. It will start at around 60%. The vapor temperature will quickly rise to around 80°C (176°F). Try to keep the temperature around this level for as long as you can by adjusting your burner. The temperature will slowly increase and the abv will slowly decrease as the run continues. Monitor your abv and keep distilling until the abv has dropped to 10%. Your vapor temperature will be around 95°C (203°F) at this point. You can distill all the way down to 0% abv, but there is not much alcohol at that point, mostly water. I recommend stopping the run at 10% abv. The entire run for a 6.5 gallon wash will take about 8 hours. I recommend having other things to do with your time during the stripping run. You just need to keep checking on the still as the run proceeds. You should collect approximately 1.5 gallons of distillate from the stripping run. This is called the "low wines." The blended abv will be around 30%. Label your collection jars with the following: Stripping Run, Batch Number, Date. Keep these in a safe place until you are ready to do the spirit run.

Collecting distillate during the stripping run.

62

Second Distillation
Spirit Run

The purpose of the spirit run is to collect and further refine the alcohol from the low wines. As discussed in chapter 1 there are several kinds of alcohol in the distillate. Our job is to separate these out and collect the ethanol which will be made into moonshine. We need to separate the run into three fractions, heads, hearts and tails. The hearts are the good stuff, ethanol, that we want to keep for drinking.

1. CLEAN YOUR STILL

After the stripping run is finished you need to clean your still. You can use alcohol or white vinegar, but don't use bleach on anything made of copper. It will corrode the copper. I recommend vinegar. Pour about a pint of vinegar into your still, add a couple of gallons of water and scrub out your still with a dish scrubber pad. Rinse out your still 3 times with a hose. Do the same for your still head. You should also pour some vinegar through you alcohol parrot and rinse it out good. The main thing you are getting rid of when cleaning your still is copper sulfate ($CuSO_4$). When you are distilling the vapors in the still contain sulfur. The sulfur binds with the copper your still is made of and creates copper sulfate. The copper sulfate binds to the interior of your still. This is a very beneficial reaction because it removes the sulfur from your distillate. This greatly improves the taste of your product. The only negative thing is you need to clean the copper sulfate out of your still after each use. Some vinegar, water and moderate scrubbing will do the job.

2. PUT A LINE OF DUCT TAPE ON YOUR TABLE

This will be for recording the temperature and abv for each of your small collection jars as the run progresses. It is important to collect the distillate in 4 ounce increments and record the temperature and abv. This will help you make the heads, hearts and tails cuts when the run is finished.

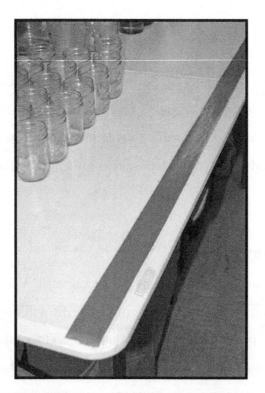

3. GET YOUR 8 OUNCE MASON JARS READY

Rinse out your jars and have them ready to go. Once the distillation gets going you will be filling jars and setting up new ones about every 10 minutes.

4. POUR THE LOW WINES INTO THE STILL

Take your low wines jars and pour them into your still. Your low wines should have an abv that is lower than 40%. If you have a batch of low wines that are higher than 40% abv you should add some purified water and dilute it down. Check the abv again with your alcohol hydrometer.

5. PUT YOUR STILL BACK TOGETHER

Put the still head back on. Connect the still head tube to the condenser. Reseal the head with flour paste.

6. TURN ON THE CONDENSER WATER LINE

You want just a trickle of water coming in through your water line. The amount coming in must equal the amount going out through the outflow line on top of the condenser. The goal is to keep the water in the condenser cool.

7. SET UP YOUR FORESHOTS COLLECTION JAR

Collect an ounce per gallon of original wash; this is your foreshots. It will contain methanol and other undesirable alcohols. For a 6 gallon wash, you would collect 6 ounces of foreshots. *Do not use your parrot to collect this first jar.* You don't want methanol in your parrot.

REMEMBER:
All of the numbers you are seeing are based on our example 10 gallon batch. You would need to adjust things for a different sized batch.

8. TURN ON YOUR BURNER

For the spirit run you can start off with medium high heat and turn it down when the temperature begins to rise to about 70ºC (158ºF).

9. COLLECT DISTILLATE (FORESHOTS)

Remember, you are not using the alcohol parrot at this step. Collect directly into your foreshots jar, the one you are going to dump. At about 60ºC (140ºF) you will start to see slow drips of distillate. It will take about half an hour for this to start. The temperature will slowly rise. Then the temperature will spike to around 78ºC (172ºF) and the speed of the drips of distillate will increase. You want a fast dripping of distillate, but not a steady steam. If you get a stream you will not be separating the different fractions of alcohol correctly. Turn the temperature down a little if this happens. When the first jar has close to 6 ounces of distillate in it get ready to pull it. I like to be on the safe side and recommend dumping 1 full ounce per gallon of wash which would be 6 ounces for our example batch. Dump the foreshots jar and check it off on your production worksheet so you know you have completed this important step.

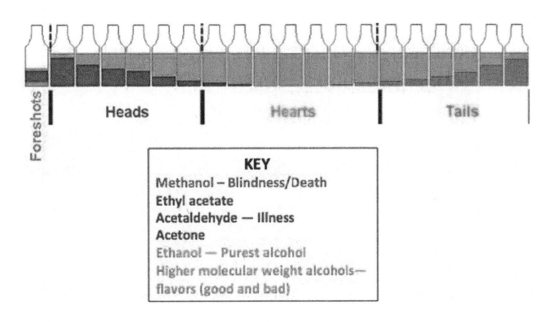

10. PUT THE ALCOHOL PARROT AND YOUR FIRST JAR IN PLACE, COLLECT DISTILLATE

After discarding the foreshots put your parrot under the distillate tube from your condenser. Put your first jar under the parrot tube to collect the distillate. It will take a few minutes for the parrot to fill with distillate and start dripping. This is helpful because it gives you some time to get your next jar in place. Put your alcohol hydrometer into the parrot. As the second jar fills your still vapor temperature will be around 80ºC (176ºF) and your abv will be around 80%. Monitor your burner and try to keep it around 80ºC (176ºF). As the run continues the temperature will slowly rise and the abv will slowly drop. Monitor your burner and adjust as necessary to keep a steady drip of distillate.

Alcohol parrot, hydrometer and collection jar in place for the spirit run.

11. CONTINUE COLLECTING 4 OUNCE QUANTITIES AND RECORDING DATA

As each jar fills to about half full, 4 ounces, replace the jar with an empty one and place the full one on your table by the duct tape. Record the temperature and abv of each jar as shown below.

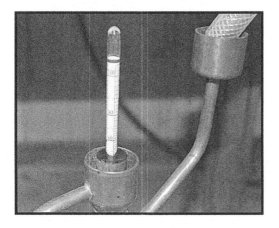 

Check the abv for each jar as they fill.   Check the vapor temperature as each jar fills.

The picture shows a jar half full of distillate with the correct data recorded on the duct tape. This one had a vapor temperature of 81°C (177.8°F) and an abv of 80%. We are dividing the run into 4 ounce increments so it will be easier the make the heads, hearts and tails cuts when the run is finished. Keep filling your jars and recording the data until the run is finished. The picture on page 76 shows you what the run will look like as it progresses.

As the run progresses your table will look the one in the picture. Each jar in a line with the temperature and abv recorded on the duct tape. You could end up with as many as 24 jars depending on when you decide to stop the run.

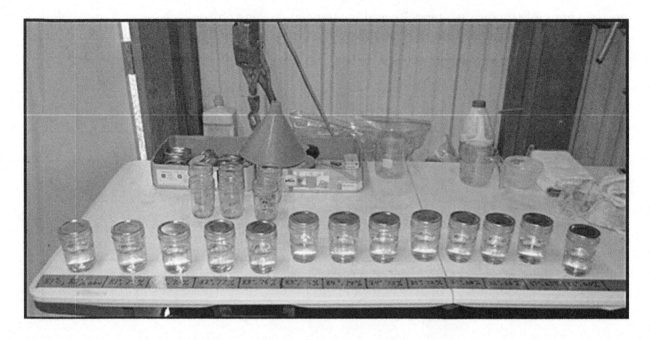

12. STOPPING THE SPIRIT RUN

There are several options for when to stop your spirit distillation run. You could continue to distill until there is zero alcohol coming out of your still, in other words, 0% abv. However, this is really not worth the effort. If you decide to distill out most of the tails in the batch and put them into your next spirit run, you could distill down to 10% abv. If you don't want to keep the tails for the next distillation, you could stop the run at the point where you think the tails have started in the run, possibly as early 65% abv if you use the 75/65 cuts. I recommend distilling until 10% abv and keeping the tails to put into the next spirit run. The reason for doing this is that there is still some ethanol in the tails that could be recovered in a subsequent run and the tails also contain esters which add unique flavors to your moonshine.

We will discuss making the cuts between heads, hearts and tails in step 13.

13. MAKING THE CUTS - HEADS, HEARTS, TAILS

Making the cuts refers to where in the spirit run you are going to make the divisions between heads, hearts and tails. There are some standard cuts that are used by commercial distillers that can be helpful in deciding where to make your cuts. The guideline I recommend is called the middle fifth cut used by the Glenmorangie Distillery in Scotland. They use a 75/65 cut. This means everything in a run that is above 75% abv is designated as heads. Everything that is below 65% abv is designated as tails. So everything from 75% to 65% abv is designated as hearts. This is considered to be a very tight cut, thereby producing a very high quality ethanol containing very little heads and very little tails. Of course, if you want a little more volume, you could use the general commercial distillery cuts of 75/55. If you do, you will need to be careful not to get to much tails in your final product or it will ruin the run. In addition to using an abv percentage there are two important considerations when making your cuts, taste and smell of the distillate. You need to smell the distillate in the jars and dip your finger in and taste them. The following information will help you with that process.

Heads

Will have a strong, fruity odor and will have a strong taste with a bite.

Contain acetone, acetaldehyde, acetate and some ethanol.

Hearts

Will smell light and sweet. They will have a smooth sweet taste.

Contain primarily ethanol - the good stuff.

Tails

Will smell light a wet dog. They will taste muddy and awful. As soon as the tails start you will be able to smell them in your distillate. Contain fusel oils including propanol, butanol and amyl alcohol. Also contain proteins, carbohydrates, fatty acids, esters and some ethanol.

After you have made your cuts and separated out your hearts you can blend in some heads and tails to adjust the flavor of your final product to your liking. It takes time to learn how to blend distillate correctly. When first learning to distill I suggest you stick with aging your hearts without any blending. After you get some experience under your belt you could start experimenting with blending.

The skill is being able to sniff out and taste where the heads end and where the tails begin. Use the 75/65 cuts as a guide. Your actual runs may come out a little different than that, but it will give you a starting point.

This picture shows the heads cut marked on the duct tape. All of the jars with an abv more than 75% will be poured into a separate container and labeled "heads." On the other end, all jars with an abv less than 65% will be poured into a separate container and labeled "tails." The heads and tails will be added to the next spirit run of the same grain bill. That way you can distill out some more of the ethanol that remains.

14. SEPARATE OUT THE HEARTS

Pour all of your small jars of hearts into a one gallon jar. Using a funnel, pour some hearts distillate into your graduated cylinder and measure the abv with your alcohol hydrometer. Next, measure the total volume in ounces using your measuring cup. Be sure to record this information in your product record. You will need this data later on if you decide to proof down (dilute) your final product.

Pouring hearts into a one gallon jar.

A funnel was used to fill the graduated cylinder with blended hearts.

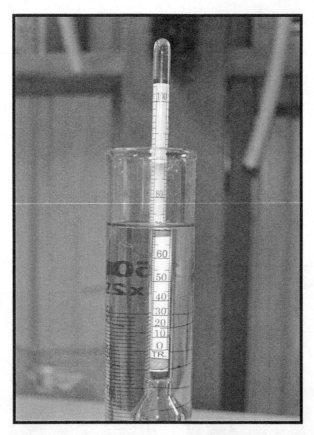

Checking the hearts abv with an alcoholometer.

Measuring the quantity of hearts with a measuring cup.

Third Distillation
2nd Spirit Run

When making moonshine a third distillation may be required to get the desired high proof spirits. Moonshiners would keep track of the distillations of a batch by placing an "X" on a jug for each distillation run. You have probably seen a moonshine jug with three X's indicating three distillations.

When doing a third distillation, follow the steps below.

1. **Pour just the hearts from the first spirit run into your still.**

2. **Add water to dilute the hearts back down to below 40% abv.**

3. **Distill like a normal spirit run.**

4. **Remove foreshots**
Remove 1 ounce per gallon of hearts being distilled. If you had a half gallon of hearts, remove 1/2 ounce of foreshots. Most of the foreshots were removed during the first spirit run, so this is all you need.

5. **Continue distilling and filling small mason jars**
Collect about 4 ounces per jar. Record temperature and abv for each jar.

6. **Distill down to where the tails are prevalent.**

7. **Make your heads and tails cuts.**
Making your cuts from the 2nd spirit run can be a little tricky. The abv may be higher because you are starting with a more purified product. The abv therefore, will not be a reliable method of making your cuts. You will need to rely more on the smell and taste of the distillate to make the cuts. The hearts should have a lightly sweet, almost neutral smell and taste.

Aging Moonshine

Strictly speaking, moonshine is not aged. However, you can age moonshine if desired. Once you age moonshine with toasted or charred wood, you technically have whiskey. You can leave it at the high proof level or proof it down to a more normal drinking level. As the distiller in charge you can do what ever you want with your distillate. In this chapter we will look at some methods of aging spirits and some of the supplies that will be needed.

AGING WOOD

Commercial distilleries age their spirits in charred oak barrels. As a home distiller you can buy small charred barrels but they are rather expensive. Another great alternative in to use charred American White Oak cubes/chunks. These are placed in an aging jar with your distillate and the aging process takes place; this method is much faster than using a barrel. Figure 3 to 6 months to properly age your spirits.

American White Oak Cubes

For jar aging you will need either toasted or charred American White Oak cubes. You can buy these at brew stores or online for about $7.00 for a 2.5 ounce package. You can also produce your own wood cubes to use for aging your moonshine and save a bunch of money. This process is covered in the next section.

Home Made White Oak Cubes

To make your own charred aging cubes buy some white oak wood, char it with a propane torch or char it on a camp stove. If you want toasted aging cubes, place the wood cubes in your oven at 400ºF for about two hours. I cut the pieces up into approximately one inch cubes. The size isn't that important as long as they will fit into your aging jar. Three one inch cubes is about the right amount for a jar of spirits. Leave the wood in until you get the color and flavor you want. You can always experiment with this. Remove the lid once a week to allow volatile vapors to escape. Or, a method I prefer, is to put three coffee filters over the jar, attach a rubber band and let it rest like that for 2 weeks. Then replace the jar cap for the remainder of the aging time.

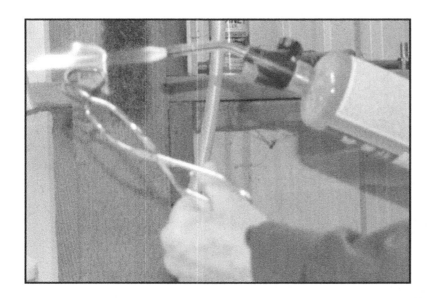

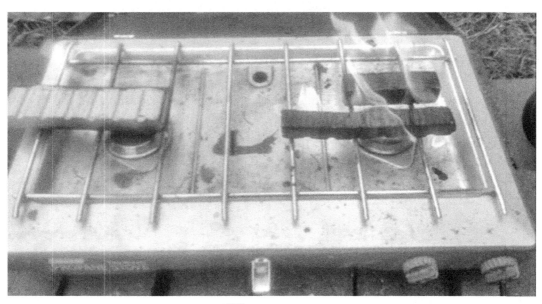

Once aging is complete, bottle your spirits. Jar aging, by placing the wood into the moonshine instead of placing the moonshine into a charred barrel, produces some excellent product in much less time. It takes about six months to produce the best product. Much less than the years it takes in a barrel. This is because you have a much greater surface area of wood per volume of moonshine in a gallon jar than you do in a barrel.

A good method to start off the aging process is to put 3 coffee filters on top of your aging jar. Leave these on for the first 2 weeks to allow volatile vapors to escape. I think this practice really improves the flavor of the moonshine.

Charring Levels and Times

Number 1 Char: 15 seconds

Number 2 Char: 30 seconds

Number 3 Char: 45 seconds

Number 4 Char: 55 seconds

Number 4 is also known as alligator char because the charred surface is rough and shiny like alligator skin.

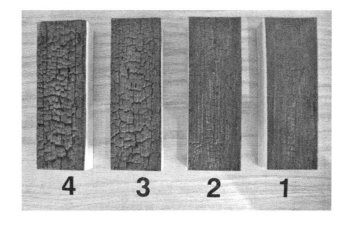

Charring causes the various components of the wood to partially break down and add to the color and flavor of the spirits it is in contact with. The main components of the wood that effect the spirits while aging are hemicellulose, lignin, tannins, and oak lactones. Once these components of the wood are charred they will interact with the spirit imparting flavors including brown sugar, caramel, toffee, vanilla, spice, wood, and coconut. The particular flavors that come through in the final spirit are determined by the level of charring and the length of time the spirit is aged with the wood.

Char #1

Char #2

Char #3

Char #4 (Alligator Char)

Bottling Moonshine

Your moonshine is ready to bottle as soon as you have identified the hearts of your spirit run. When the time arrives, get out your bottles, your funnel and some coffee filters.

1. PROOF YOUR MOONSHINE DOWN TO THE DRINKING PROOF YOU WANT - IF DESIRED

Decide what proof you want for your moonshine, 80, 90, etc., or just leave it the way it is. Measure the volume of moonshine in your jar. Use the dilution calculator at **http://homedistiller.org/calcs/rad14701**. Plug in the numbers and it will tell you how much water to add to your moonshine for the proof your want. Use purified water for proofing down.

2. RINSE OUT YOUR BOTTLES (EVEN NEW ONES)

3. FILTER YOUR MOONSHINE INTO THE BOTTLE

4. PUT THE CORK IN

5. ATTACH YOUR LABEL

I recommend designing a label on your computer with MS Publisher. Print the label on plain paper. Cut it out and glue it onto your bottle using a glue stick. The glue stick works well and it is easy to remove the label when you need to recycle any bottles. See the example on page 81.

Using nice bottles makes your
moonshine look even better!

Filtering moonshine into a bottle using a
funnel and coffee filter.

CLASSIC MOONSHINE
WORKSHEET

Grain Bill and Recipe   Batch No. _____   Batch Name_____

This recipe will produce a 10 gallon mash. You can easily alter the quantities to produce a smaller or larger batch if desired.

Water - 8 Gallons
Corn Meal - 85%, 20.4 lb.
Barley Malt - 15%, 3.6 lb.
Alpha-amylase Enzyme - 1 tsp
Fermax Yeast Nutrient - 10 tsp
Yeast - 5 tsp

Cooking the Mash

1. **Put 8 gallons of water in your cooking pot (✓) _____**   **Date _____**

2. **Heat to 75°C (167°F) _____**

3. **Add the corn meal and allow to gelatinize for 1 hour _____**

4. **Allow temperature to drop to 64°C (148°F) _____**

5. **Mix in the alpha-amylase enzyme _____**

6. **Mix in the barley malt _____**

7. **Check the pH (want 5.2-5.8) _____   Adjusted pH _____**

8. **Put the lid on and rest the mash for 90 minutes at 64°C (148°F) _____**

9. **Cool the mash to 75-80°F _____**

10. **Check the specific gravity of the wort. OG _____   PA _____**

Notes:
_____
_____

Fermentation

Date _____ Time _____

1. Sanitize fermentation equipment _____

2. Secure mash bag in fermenter _____

3. Check to make sure the mash temperature is around 75-80°F _____

4. Check the mash pH (want 4.0-4.5) _____   Adjusted pH _____

5. Add yeast nutrients, mix _____

6. Pitch yeast, mix _____

7. Aerate the mash _____

8. Pour mash into fermenter _____

9. Put the lid on fermenter and label - Batch number, date, time, OG _____

10. Place fermenter in fermentation room _____

11. Set heater temperature to 75-80°F _____

Procedures During Fermentation

1. Check for grain cap and crackling sound _____

2. Check the temperature of the fermentation room _____

3. Check the specific gravity of the wash:

    1st SG Check: Date _____ SG _____

    2nd SG Check: Date _____ SG _____

    Terminal Gravity: Date _____ TG _____ PA _____

    Net PA _____

Notes:
_____
_____
_____

Recovering the Wash

1. Open the fermenter and tie a rope around the top of the mash bag _____

2. Pull the mash bag out of the fermenter _____

3. Allow the mash bag to drain: Number of hours _____ or Overnight _____

4. Press out the remaining wash _____

5. Allow the wash to settle for 2 days _____

Stripping Run

Heat slowly. Run to 96°F or 10% abv. Approximately 8 hours. Low Wines.

Date _____   Start Time _____   End Time _____

1. Remove the wash from the fermenter _____

2. Pour the wash into the still _____

3. Attach still head and fasten condenser tube _____

4. Seal the still head _____

5. Set up 1 gallon collection jar and alcohol parrot _____

6. Turn on the burner - medium heat to start _____

7. Turn on condenser water line _____

8. Collect distillate _____

    First Drips: Time _____ Distillate Temperature _____

    Fast Drips: Time _____ Distillate Temperature _____

    Starting abv _____   Time _____   Distillate Temperature _____

    Ending abv _____   Time _____   Distillate Temperature _____

    Final Blended abv _____   Quantity _____

84

Spirit Run				

Date __-____   Start Time _____

Low Wines abv _____   Water Added _____   Adjusted abv _____

Foreshots Amount Collected _____   Dumped _____

Jar No.	Time	Temp	abv	Notes

85

Jar No.	Time	Temp	abv	Notes

Spirit Run Data

Heads Cut: abv _____   Temperature _____

Tails Cut: abv _____   Temperature _____

Total Volume: _____   abv _____

Hearts Volume: _____   abv _____

Aging

Start Date _____   End Date _____

Quantity _____   abv _____   Aging Proof _____

Barrel _____   Toasted Wood Chips _____   Charred Wood Chips _____

Bottling

Date _____   Volume _____   Bottled Proof _____

Notes:
_____
_____

Chapter 4
Additional Moonshine Recipes

Technically speaking, moonshine is any illegally produced spirit with a high alcohol content. Moonshine per se, is a high-proof, clear, unaged whiskey. Moonshiner's will usually distill their moonshine 3 times in order to reach a high proof level. Traditional moonshine is made of corn and sugar, or corn and barley malt. The thing to keep in mind is you can make moonshine out of anything you want. I have included some standard moonshine recipes in this section. I recommend aiming for an original gravity of about 1.080 (target gravity) and potential alcohol of about 10%. This would indicate a good sugar content and potential alcohol level, and will not stress your yeast. Excessive sugar content in a mash or an excessive alcohol content in a fermenting wort can stress or even kill your yeast. This can lead to off flavors or a stuck fermentation. Some distillers will go higher than 1.080, but I think it is a safe level that produces a good volume of spirits. If you do cook a mash that goes a little beyond that level it isn't a big deal. Each of the following moonshine recipes requires 8 gallons of water and 24 pounds of grain, or a combination of grain and sugar. They will make about 10 gallons of mash and produce about 3 fifths of finished product. The higher your proof, the lower your yield will be. For these moonshine recipes follow the specific mashing directions for each recipe. Many of the procedures are the same as for the Classic Moonshine recipe, but there are some variations between recipes. Use the appropriate worksheets that are recommended for each recipe.

CORN MEAL MOONSHINE

Water - 8 gallons
Corn meal - 12 lb.
Sugar - 12 lb.
Alpha-amylase enzyme - 1 tsp
Glucoamylase enzyme - 1 tsp
Fermax yeast nutrient - 10 tsp
Yeast - 5 tsp

COOKING THE MASH

1. PUT 8 GALLONS OF WATER INTO YOUR COOKING POT

2. HEAT THE WATER TO 75°C (167°F).

3. ADD THE CORN MEAL AND GELATINIZE FOR 1 HOUR

For any grain bill that includes corn, the corn must be gelatinized. Put in 12 lb. of corn meal. Stir constantly as you add the corn or you will get corn dough balls that are hard to mix in. Once it is well mixed, put the lid on the pot and let it sit for one hour. You want to keep the temperature between 70°C (158°F) and 75°C (167°F). The corn mash will get very thick. It will liquefy after you mix in the alpha-amylase enzyme later on.

4. ALLOW THE TEMPERATURE TO DROP TO 64°C (148°F)

5. ADD THE ALPHA-AMYLASE ENZYME

Mix in the enzyme. This will liquify the gelatinized corn.

6. ADD THE SUGAR

Mix in the sugar. Add heat to keep the temperature at 64°C (148°F).

7. CHECK THE MASH pH

Take a sample of wort, allow it to drop to room temperature, and check the pH. You want between 5.2 and 5.8. Adjust as necessary.

8. REST THE MASH FOR 90 MINUTES

Put the lid on the pot and allow to rest. Saccharification is occurring in this step. Keep temperature at 64°C (148°F). If ambient temperature is cold, wrap the pot with a blanket.

9. ADD THE GLUCOAMYLASE ENZYME

After 90 minutes has passed, allow the mash to cool to 140°F. Then add the glucoamylase enzyme and mix it in. Allow to rest for 1 hour. Glucoamylase will also help break down starches , primarily dextrins, into fermentable sugars during fermentation.

10. COOL THE MASH TO 75-80°F

Use a wort chiller or let the mash rest over night to cool.

11. CHECK THE SPECIFIC GRAVITY OF THE WORT

Once the wort has cooled to between 24 and 27°C (75 and 80°F), place your kitchen strainer into the mash bucket to separate some wort from the grain. Using your turkey baster draw some wort and place it into your graduated cylinder. Fill it to within about 3 inches of the top. Use your saccharometer to check the specific gravity of the wort. It should read somewhere around 1.080 which equates to a potential alcohol of 10.5%. Your actual SG could be a little less or a little more. This will be your original gravity (OG). Your potential alcohol (PA) should be between 8 and 11%. Every batch will vary by a small amount. Not to worry. If your gravity too low for some reason, you can add more sugar. See page 121 for instructions on adding sugar. If your gravity is too high, you can add some water to drop it down. Just add a cup at a time, mix it up, recheck the gravity. The target is 1.080, but it doesn't have to be exact. Record your OG and PA in your distillation worksheet (record).

WORKSHEETS

For fermentation through bottling, use the instructions for making Classic Moonshine in chapter 3, pages 52-80. The same procedures can be used for making corn meal moonshine.

For cooking the mash, photocopy and use the worksheet on the next page.
For fermentation through bottling, photocopy and use the classic moonshine worksheets, pages 83-86, the procedures are the same.

CORN MEAL MOONSHINE
WORKSHEET

Grain Bill and Recipe   Batch No. _____   Batch Name_____

Water - 8 Gallons

Corn meal - 12 lb.

Sugar - 12 lb.

Alpha-amylase enzyme - 1 tsp

Glucoamylase enzyme - 1 tsp

Fermax yeast nutrient - 10 tsp

Yeast - 5 tsp

Cooking the Mash

1. Put 8 gallons of water in your cooking pot (✓) _____   Date _____

2. Heat water to 75°C (167°F) _____

3. Add the corn meal and allow to gelatinize for 1 hour _____

4. Allow temperature to drop to 64°C (148°F) _____

5. Mix in the alpha-amylase enzyme _____

6. Mix in the sugar _____

7. Check the pH (want 5.2-5.8) _____   Adjusted pH _____

8. Put the lid on and rest the mash for 90 minutes at 64°C (148°F) _____

9. Mix in the glucoamylase enzyme when the temperature drops to 60°C (140°F) _____

10. Cool the mash to 24-27°C (75-80°F) _____

11. Check the specific gravity of the wort. OG _____   PA _____

Notes:
_____
_____
_____
_____

CRACKED CORN MOONSHINE

Cracked corn has a lower specific gravity when mashed than either flaked corn or corn meal. It comes in at about 1.030. Cracked corn needs to be ground finer in order to expose more of the starch. I use a grain grinder and run cracked corn through it twice. I also find that allowing the cracked corn to rest longer in the cooking pot during mashing will help in the saccharification process and produce a higher OG. Leaving it to rest overnight is helpful.

Water - 8 gallons
Cracked corn - 12 lb.
Sugar - 12 lb.
Alpha-amylase enzyme - 1 tsp
Glucoamylase enzyme - 1 tsp
Fermax yeast nutrient - 10 tsp
Yeast - 5 tsp

COOKING THE MASH

1. PUT 8 GALLONS OF WATER INTO YOUR COOKING POT

2. HEAT THE WATER TO 75°C (167°F).

3. ADD THE CRACKED CORN AND GELATINIZE FOR 1 HOUR

For any grain bill that includes corn, the corn must be gelatinized. Put in 12 lb. of cracked corn. Stir constantly as you add the corn or you will get corn dough balls that are hard to mix in. Once it is well mixed, put the lid on the pot and let it sit for one hour or more if needed. You want to keep the temperature between 70°C (158°F) and 75°C (167°F). The corn mash will get very thick. It will liquefy after you mix in the alpha-amylase enzyme later on.

4. ALLOW THE TEMPERATURE TO DROP TO 148°F

5. ADD THE ALPHA-AMYLASE ENZYME

Mix in the enzyme. This will liquify the gelatinized corn.

6. ADD THE SUGAR

Mix in the sugar until dissolved.

7. CHECK THE MASH pH

Take a sample of wort, allow it to drop to room temperature, and check the pH. You want between 5.2 and 5.8. Adjust as necessary.

8. REST THE MASH FOR 90 MINUTES

Cover the pot and allow to rest. Saccharification is occurring in this step. Keep temperature at 64°C (148°F). If ambient temperature is cold, wrap the pot with a blanket.

9. ADD THE GLUCOAMYLASE ENZYME

After 90 minutes has passed, allow the mash to cool to 140°F. Then add the glucoamylase enzyme and mix it in. Allow to rest for 1 hour. Glucoamylase will also help break down starches , primarily dextrins, into fermentable sugars during fermentation.

10. COOL THE MASH TO 75-80°F

Use a wort chiller or let the mash rest over night to cool.

11. CHECK THE SPECIFIC GRAVITY OF THE WORT

Once the wort has cooled to between 24 and 27°C (75 and 80°F), place your kitchen strainer into the mash bucket to separate some wort from the grain. Using your turkey baster draw some wort and place it into your graduated cylinder. Fill it to within about 3 inches of the top. Use your saccharometer to check the specific gravity of the wort. It should read somewhere around 1.080 which equates to a potential alcohol of 10.5%. Your actual SG could be a little less or a little more. This will be your original gravity (OG). Your potential alcohol (PA) should be between 8 and 11%. Every batch will vary by a small amount. Not to worry. If your gravity too low for some reason, you can add more sugar. See page 121 for instructions on adding sugar. If your gravity is too high, you can add some water to drop it down. Just add a cup at a time, mix it up, recheck the gravity. The target is 1.080, but it doesn't have to be exact. Record your OG and PA in your distillation worksheet (record).

WORKSHEETS

For fermentation through bottling, use the instructions for making Classic Moonshine in chapter 3, pages 52-80. The same procedures can be used for making cracked corn moonshine.

For cooking the mash, photocopy and use the worksheet on the next page.
For fermentation through bottling, photocopy and use the classic moonshine worksheets, pages 83-86, the procedures are the same.

CRACKED CORN MOONSHINE WORKSHEET

Grain Bill and Recipe   Batch No. _____ Batch Name_____

Water - 8 Gallons

Cracked corn - 12 lb.

Sugar - 12 lb.

Alpha-amylase enzyme - 1 tsp

Glucoamylase enzyme - 1 tsp

Fermax yeast nutrient - 10 tsp

Yeast - 5 tsp

Cooking the Mash

1. **Put 8 gallons of water in your cooking pot (✓) _____   Date _____**

2. **Heat water to 75°C (167°F) _____**

3. **Add the cracked corn and allow to gelatinize for 1 hour or more _____**

4. **Allow temperature to drop to 64°C (148°F) _____**

5. **Mix in the alpha-amylase enzyme _____**

6. **Mix in the sugar _____**

7. **Check the pH (want 5.2-5.8) _____   Adjusted pH _____**

8. **Put the lid on and rest the mash for 90 minutes at 64°C (148°F) _____**

9. **Mix in the glucoamylase enzyme when the temperature drops to 60°C (140°F) _____**

10. **Cool the mash to 24-27°C (75-80°F) _____**

11. **Check the specific gravity of the wort. OG _____ PA _____**

Notes:
_____
_____
_____
_____

MALTED BARLEY MOONSHINE

Water- 8 gallons
Barley malt - 20 lb.
Sugar - 4 lb.
Alpha-amylase enzyme - 1 tsp
Fermax yeast nutrient - 10 tsp
Yeast - 1 tsp

COOKING THE MASH

1. PUT 8 GALLONS OF WATER INTO YOUR COOKING POT

2. HEAT THE WATER TO 64°C (148°F)

3. ADD THE BARLEY MALT
Mix in well.

4. ADD THE ALPHA-AMYLASE ENZYME
Mix in the enzyme. The alpha-amylase, plus the enzymes in the barley malt, will convert the starches into fermentable sugars.

5. ADD THE SUGAR
Mix in the sugar until dissolved.

6. CHECK THE MASH pH
Take a sample of wort, allow it to drop to room temperature, and check the pH. You want between 5.2 and 5.8. Adjust as necessary.

7. REST THE MASH FOR 90 MINUTES
Cover the pot and allow to rest. Saccharification is occurring in this step. Keep temperature at 64°C (148°F). If ambient temperature is cold, wrap the pot with a blanket.

8. COOL THE MASH TO 75-80°F
Use a wort chiller or let the mash rest over night to cool.

9. CHECK THE SPECIFIC GRAVITY OF THE WORT

Once the wort has cooled to between 24 and 27ºC (75 and 80ºF), place your kitchen strainer into the mash bucket to separate some wort from the grain. Using your turkey baster draw some wort and place it into your graduated cylinder. Fill it to within about 3 inches of the top. Use your saccharometer to check the specific gravity of the wort. It should read somewhere around 1.080 which equates to a potential alcohol of 10.5%. Your actual SG could be a little less or a little more. This will be your original gravity (OG). Your potential alcohol (PA) should be between 8 and 11%. Every batch will vary by a small amount. Not to worry. If your gravity too low for some reason, you can add more sugar. See page 121 for instructions on adding sugar. If your gravity is too high, you can add some water to drop it down. Just add a cup at a time, mix it up, recheck the gravity. The target is 1.080, but it doesn't have to be exact. Record your OG and PA in your distillation worksheet (record).

WORKSHEETS

For fermentation through bottling, use the instructions for making Classic Moonshine in chapter 3, pages 52-80. The same procedures can be used for making malted barley moonshine.

For cooking the mash, photocopy and use the worksheet on the next page.
For fermentation through bottling, photocopy and use the classic moonshine worksheets, pages 83-86, the procedures are the same.

MALTED BARLEY MOONSHINE
WORKSHEET

Grain Bill and Recipe   Batch No. _____ Batch Name_____

Water- 8 gallons

Barley malt - 20 lb.

Sugar - 4 lb.

Alpha-amylase enzyme - 1 tsp

Fermax yeast nutrient - 10 tsp

Yeast - 1 tsp

Cooking the Mash

1. **Put 8 gallons of water in your cooking pot (✓) _____   Date _____**

2. **Heat the water to 64°C (148°F) _____**

3. **Mix in the malted barley _____**

4. **Mix in the alpha-amylase enzyme _____**

5. **Mix in the sugar _____**

6. **Check the pH (want 5.2-5.8) _____ Adjusted pH _____**

7. **Put the lid on and rest the mash for 90 minutes at 64°C (148°F) _____**

8. **Cool the mash to 24-27°C (75-80°F) _____**

9. **Check the specific gravity of the wort. OG _____ PA _____**

Notes:
_____
_____
_____
_____

OATMEAL MOONSHINE RECIPE

Water - 8 Gallons
Oats - rolled or flaked - 15 lb.
Barley malt - 4 lb.
Brown sugar - 5 lb.
Amylase enzyme - 1 tsp
Fermax yeast nutrients - 5 tsp
Yeast - 5 tsp

COOKING THE MASH

1. PUT 8 GALLONS OF WATER INTO YOUR COOKING POT

2. HEAT THE WATER TO 64°C (148°F)

3. ADD THE OATS AND BARLEY MALT

4. ADD THE ALPHA-AMYLASE ENZYME

Mix in the enzyme. The alpha-amylase, plus the enzymes in the barley malt, will convert the starches into fermentable sugars.

5. ADD THE BROWN SUGAR

Mix in the sugar until dissolved.

6. CHECK THE MASH pH

Take a sample of wort, allow it to drop to room temperature, and check the pH. You want between 5.2 and 5.8. Adjust as necessary.

7. REST THE MASH FOR 90 MINUTES

Cover the pot and allow to rest. Saccharification is occurring in this step. Keep temperature at 64°C (148°F). If ambient temperature is cold, wrap the pot with a blanket.

8. COOL THE MASH TO 75-80°F

Use a wort chiller or let the mash rest over night to cool.

9. CHECK THE SPECIFIC GRAVITY OF THE WORT

Once the wort has cooled to between 24 and 27°C (75 and 80°F), place your kitchen strainer into the mash bucket to separate some wort from the grain. Using your turkey baster draw some wort and place it into your graduated cylinder. Fill it to within about 3 inches of the top. Use your saccharometer to check the specific gravity of the wort. It should read somewhere around 1.080 which equates to a potential alcohol of 10.5%. Your actual SG could be a little less or a little more. This will be your original gravity (OG). Your potential alcohol (PA) should be between 8 and 11%. Every batch will vary by a small amount. Not to worry. If your gravity too low for some reason, you can add more sugar. See page 121 for instructions on adding sugar. If your gravity is too high, you can add some water to drop it down. Just add a cup at a time, mix it up, recheck the gravity. The target is 1.080, but it doesn't have to be exact. Record your OG and PA in your distillation worksheet (record).

WORKSHEETS

For fermentation through bottling, use the instructions for making Classic Moonshine in chapter 3, pages 52-80. The same procedures can be used for making oatmeal moonshine.

For cooking the mash, photocopy and use the worksheet on the next page. For fermentation through bottling, photocopy and use the classic moonshine worksheets, pages 83-86, the procedures are the same.

OATMEAL MOONSHINE
WORKSHEET

Grain Bill and Recipe   Batch No. _____ Batch Name_____

Water - 8 Gallons
Oats - rolled or flaked - 15 lb.
Barley malt - 4 lb.
Brown sugar - 5 lb.
Amylase enzyme - 1 tsp
Fermax yeast nutrients - 5 tsp

Cooking the Mash

1. **Put 8 gallons of water in your cooking pot (✓) _____   Date _____**

2. **Heat the water to 64°C (148°F) _____**

3. **Mix in the oats and malted barley _____**

4. **Mix in the alpha-amylase enzyme _____**

5. **Mix in the brown sugar _____**

6. **Check the pH (want 5.2-5.8) _____   Adjusted pH _____**

7. **Put the lid on and rest the mash for 90 minutes at 64°C (148°F) _____**

8. **Cool the mash to 24-27°C (75-80°F) _____**

9. **Check the specific gravity of the wort. OG _____   PA _____**

Notes:
_____
_____
_____
_____

APPLE MOONSHINE

Ripe Apples - 5 lb.

Apple juice - 5 gallons

White sugar - 3¾ lb.

Pectic enzyme - 3 tsp

Fermax yeast nutrient - 6 tsp

Lalvin EC-1118 Champagne yeast - 2 tsp

Makes about a 6 gallon batch

> **FYI**
> *You should get about 3 fifths of 80 proof apple moonshine from this recipe; less if you keep the proof higher.*

COOKING THE MASH

1. CUT UP THE APPLES

I like to cut them into fourths. This works well with a fruit crusher. If you are going to use a food processor or some kind of blender, you might want to cut them in eighths. I like to mash the entire apple; core, stem, everything. It all gets strained out in the end.

2. CRUSH THE APPLES

I use a fruit crusher for this process - it works really well, plus you get a bit of a workout.

3. PUT THE CRUSHED APPLES AND JUICE INTO THE COOKING POT

4. COOK THE APPLES AND THE JUICE

Place the apples and juice in your cooking pot. Heat to a low boil and allow to simmer with the lid on for 30 minutes.

5. MASH UP THE APPLES IN THE JUICE

Use a large potato masher to mash up the apples with the juice.

6. ADD THE SUGAR

Mix the sugar until it is dissolved.

7. CHECK THE SPECIFIC GRAVITY OF THE WORT

Once the wort has cooled to between 24 and 27°C (75 and 80°F), place your kitchen strainer into the mash bucket to separate some wort from the grain. Using your turkey baster draw some wort and place it into your graduated cylinder. Fill it to within about 3 inches of the top. Use your saccharometer to check the specific gravity of the wort. It should read somewhere around 1.080 which equates to a potential alcohol of 10.5%. Your actual SG could be a little less or a little more. This will be your original gravity (OG). Your potential alcohol (PA) should be between 8 and 11%. Every batch will vary by a small amount. Not to worry. If your gravity too low for some reason, you can add more sugar. See page 121 for instructions on adding sugar. If your gravity is too high, you can add some water to drop it down. Just add a cup at a time, mix it up, recheck the gravity. The target is 1.080, but it doesn't have to be exact. Record your OG and PA in your distillation worksheet (record).

8. ALLOW THE MASH TO COOL DOWN TO ABOUT 27°C (80°F)

9. ADD THE PECTIC ENZYME

Mix in the pectic enzyme. Make sure your mash temperature is down to about 27°C (80°F) before adding the pectic enzyme. Higher temperatures can decrease the effectiveness of the enzyme. Pectic enzyme will help break down the pectin, especially in the pulp, and produce more juice.

FERMENTATION

Fermentation for fruit mash should be complete in 4 to 6 days. If fermentation stops, stuck fermentation, add another half dose of nutrients, mix it up, and let it continue fermenting until TG, or close to it, is reached.

1. SANITIZE FERMENTATION EQUIPMENT
See chapter 6.

2. SECURE MASH BAG INTO THE FERMENTER

3. CHECK THE WASH TEMPERATURE
Should be 24°C-27°C (75°F-80°F). Adjust if necessary.

4. CHECK THE pH OF THE JUICE

The pH of your apple juice wash should be between 4.0-4.5. If it is too low add calcium carbonate to raise it. If it is too high add citric acid to lower it. Add a teaspoon at a time, mix it in good, and recheck the pH. Keep adding more until the pH is where it should be. See pH in the expanded glossary for more in depth information.

5. ADD THE YEAST NUTRIENTS

Mix in the nutrients. Although apples provide a good deal of nutrients to the yeast, I still recommend using some nutrients to make <u>sure</u> they are well fed. Healthy yeast produce good quality alcohol.

6. PITCH THE YEAST

We are using EC-1118 Champagne yeast for this recipe. Champagne yeast is popular for fermenting fruit juice, but there are other strains of yeast you can also use. Make a yeast starter by getting a cup of 43°C (110°F) water. Add a tsp of sugar. Add the required amount of yeast. Mix it up and let it sit for about 15 minutes. The yeast will hydrate and start becoming active. active. Once you see a couple of inches of barm (foam) on top of the water it is ready to pitch. Make sure the wash has cooled down to about 27°C (80°F). Pour the yeast starter into your fruit wash, mix everything well.

7. AERATE THE WASH

Pour the wash between two 5 gallon buckets 3 times. I fill a bucket about half way with wash, pour it back and forth 3 times, then pour it into the fermenter. You could also use an aquarium pump to aerate - much easier method. The yeast need the oxygen during the lag phase of fermentation - don't skip this step.

8. POUR THE WASH INTO THE FERMENTER

9. PUT THE LID ON THE FERMENTER AND LABEL IT

10. PLACE THE FERMENTER IN YOUR FERMENTATION ROOM

11. SET THE ROOM TEMPERATURE TO 24-27°C (75-80°F)

PROCEDURES DURING FERMENTATION

1. CHECK FOR THE BUBBLING AND FIZZING SOUND

2. MONITOR THE TEMPERATURE OF YOUR FERMENTATION ROOM

3. CHECK THE SG EVERY COUPLE OF DAYS UNTIL THE TG IS REACHED

WORKSHEETS

For recovering the wash through bottling, use the instructions for making Classic Moonshine in chapter 3, pages 56-80. The same procedures can be used for making apple moonshine.

For cooking the mash, fermentation, and procedures during fermentation photocopy and use the worksheets on the next two pages.

For recovering the wash through bottling, photocopy and use the classic moonshine worksheets, pages 84-86, the procedures are the same.

APPLE MOONSHINE
WORKSHEET

Grain Bill and Recipe   Batch No. _____ Batch Name_____

Ripe Apples - 5 lb.

Apple juice - 5 gallons

White sugar - 3¾ lb.

Pectic enzyme - 3 tsp

Fermax yeast nutrient - 6 tsp

Lalvin EC-1118 Champagne yeast - 2 tsp

Cooking the Mash

1. **Cut up the apples (✓)** _____   Date _____

2. **Crush the apples** _____

3. **Put the crushed apple and the juice into the cooking pot** _____

4. **Cook the apples in the juice, simmer for 30 minutes** _____

5. **Mash up the apples in the juice** _____

6. **Mix in the sugar** _____

7. **Check the specific gravity of the juice OG _____ PA _____**

8. **Allow the juice to cool to about 27°C (80°F)** _____

9. **Add the pectic enzyme** _____

Notes:
_____
_____
_____
_____

Fermentation

Date _____ Time _____

1. Sanitize fermentation equipment _____

2. Secure mash bag in fermenter _____

3. Check to make sure the mash temperature is around 24-27°C (75-80°F) _____

4. Check the juice pH (want 4.0-4.5) _____ Adjusted pH _____

5. Add yeast nutrients, mix _____

6. Pitch yeast, mix _____

7. Aerate the mash _____

8. Pour mash into fermenter _____

9. Put the lid on fermenter and label - Batch number, date, time, OG _____

10. Place fermenter in fermentation room _____

11. Set heater temperature to 24-27°C (75-80°F) _____

Procedures During Fermentation

1. Check for the bubbling and fizzing sound _____

2. Check the temperature of the fermentation room _____

3. Check the specific gravity of the wash:

    1st SG Check: Date _____ SG _____

    2nd SG Check: Date _____ SG _____

    Terminal Gravity: Date _____ TG _____ PA _____

    Net PA _____

Notes:
_____
_____
_____

WATERMELON MOONSHINE

For this watermelon moonshine recipe we keep all of the juice and pomace (skin, seeds, pulp) together, so it is more of a mash. We will be using a fair amount of water, and sugar to help increase the volume of moonshine we produce.

This will make a 7 gallon fruit mash.

Water - 2 gallons

Watermelons - 3 large, (about 20 lbs. each)

  - this should produce about 13 pounds of actual fruit and about 4 gallons of juice/pulp.

White Sugar - 8 pounds (adds about 1 gal. to total mash volume)

Pectic Enzyme - 3½ tsp

Fermax yeast nutrient - 7 tsp

Lalvin EC-1118 Champagne yeast - 2½ tsp

COOKING THE MASH

1. SLICE THE WATERMELONS AND CUT UP INTO SMALL CHUNKS

Cut up the watermelons into pieces, 2x2" or so. Just the fruit, don't need the rind.

2. PUT THE WATERMELON CHUNKS AND JUICE INTO THE COOKING POT

3. ADD THE WATER

An RV water filter works well for filtering your mash water.

4. COOK ON LOW BOIL FOR 30 MINUTES

Keep the lid on the pot. Stir up the mash every few minutes to help it heat evenly. Cooking the mash will sterilize it and help break down the pulp and produce more fermentable juice.

5. MASH THE COOKED WATERMELON

Use a large potato masher to mash the cooked watermelon.

6. ADD SUGAR

Mix the sugar in until dissolved.

7. CHECK THE SPECIFIC GRAVITY OF THE WORT

Once the wort has cooled to between 24 and 27°C (75 and 80°F), place your kitchen strainer into the mash bucket to separate some wort from the grain. Using your turkey baster draw some wort and place it into your graduated cylinder. Fill it to within about 3 inches of the top. Use your saccharometer to check the specific gravity of the wort. It should read somewhere around 1.080 which equates to a potential alcohol of 10.5%. Your actual SG could be a little less or a little more. This will be your original gravity (OG). Your potential alcohol (PA) should be between 8 and 11%. Every batch will vary by a small amount. Not to worry. If your gravity too low for some reason, you can add more sugar. See page 121 for instructions on adding sugar. If your gravity is too high, you can add some water to drop it down. Just add a cup at a time, mix it up, recheck the gravity. The target is 1.080, but it doesn't have to be exact. Record your OG and PA in your distillation worksheet (record).

8. ALLOW THE MASH TO COOL DOWN TO ABOUT 27°C (80°F)

9. ADD PECTIC ENZYME

Mix in the pectic enzyme. Make sure your mash temperature is down to about 27°C (80°F) before adding the pectic enzyme. Higher temperatures can decrease the effectiveness of the enzyme. Pectic enzyme will help break down the pectin, especially in the pulp, and produce more juice.

FERMENTATION

Fermentation for fruit mash should be complete in 4 to 6 days. If fermentation stops, stuck fermentation, add another half dose of nutrients, mix it up, and let it continue fermenting until TG, or close to it, is reached.

1. SANITIZE FERMENTATION EQUIPMENT
See chapter 6.

2. SECURE MASH BAG INTO THE FERMENTER

3. CHECK THE WASH TEMPERATURE
Should be 24°C-27°C (75°F-80°F). Adjust if necessary.

4. CHECK THE pH OF THE WASH

The pH of your watermelon juice wash should be between 4.0-4.5. If it is too low add calcium carbonate to raise it. If it is too high add citric acid to lower it. Add a ½ tsp at a time, mix it in good, and recheck the pH. Keep adding more until the pH is where it should be. See pH in the expanded glossary for more in depth information.

5. ADD THE YEAST NUTRIENTS

Mix in the nutrients. Although apples provide a good deal of nutrients to the yeast, I still recommend using some nutrients to make <u>sure</u> they are well fed. Healthy yeast produce good quality alcohol.

6. PITCH THE YEAST

We are using EC-1118 Champagne yeast for this recipe. Champagne yeast is popular for fermenting fruit juice, but there are other strains of yeast you can also use. Make a yeast starter by getting a cup of 43°C (110°F) water. Add a tsp of sugar. Add the required amount of yeast. Mix it up and let it sit for about 15 minutes. The yeast will hydrate and start becoming active. active. Once you see a couple of inches of barm (foam) on top of the water it is ready to pitch. Make sure the wash has cooled down to about 27°C (80°F). Pour the yeast starter into your fruit wash, mix everything well.

7. AERATE THE WASH

Pour the wash between two 5 gallon buckets 3 times. I fill a bucket about half way with wash, pour it back and forth 3 times, then pour it into the fermenter. You could also use an aquarium pump to aerate - much easier method. The yeast need the oxygen during the lag phase of fermentation - don't skip this step.

8. POUR THE WASH INTO THE FERMENTER

9. PUT THE LID ON THE FERMENTER AND LABEL IT

10. PLACE THE FERMENTER IN YOUR FERMENTATION ROOM

11. SET THE ROOM TEMPERATURE TO 24-27°C (75-80°F)

PROCEDURES DURING FERMENTATION

1. **CHECK FOR THE BUBBLING AND FIZZING SOUND**

2. **MONITOR THE TEMPERATURE OF YOUR FERMENTATION ROOM**

3. **CHECK THE SG EVERY COUPLE OF DAYS UNTIL THE TG IS REACHED**

WORKSHEETS

For recovering the wash through bottling, use the instructions for making Classic Moonshine in chapter 3, pages 56-80. The same procedures can be used for making watermelon moonshine.

For cooking the mash, fermentation, and procedures during fermentation photocopy and use the worksheets on the next two pages.

For recovering the wash through bottling, photocopy and use the classic moonshine worksheets, pages 84-86, the procedures are the same.

WATERMELON MOONSHINE
WORKSHEET

Recipe	Batch No. _____	Batch Name _____

Water - 2 gallons

Watermelons - 3 large, ripe, about 20 pounds of fruit, about 4 gallons of juice and pomace.

White sugar - 7.8 lb.

Pectic enzyme - 3½ tsp

Fermax yeast nutrient - 7 tsp

Lalvin EC-1118 Champagne yeast - 2 tsp

Cooking the Mash

1. Slice the watermelon and cut into small chunks _____   Date _____

3. Put the watermelon chunks into the cooking pot _____

4. Add the water _____

5. Cook on low boil for 30 minutes _____

6. Mash the cooked watermelon _____

6. Mix in the sugar _____

7. Check the specific gravity of the juice OG _____ PA _____

8. Allow to cool down to about 27°C (80°F) _____

9. Add the pectic enzyme _____

Notes:
_____
_____
_____
_____

Fermentation

Date _____ Time _____

1. Sanitize fermentation equipment _____

2. Secure mash bag in fermenter _____

3. Check to make sure the mash temperature is around 24-27°C (75-80°F) _____

4. Check the juice pH (want 4.0-4.5) _____ Adjusted pH _____

5. Add yeast nutrients, mix _____

6. Pitch yeast, mix _____

7. Aerate the mash _____

8. Pour mash into fermenter _____

9. Put the lid on fermenter and label - Batch number, date, time, OG _____

10. Place fermenter in fermentation room _____

11. Set heater temperature to 24-27°C (75-80°F) _____

Procedures During Fermentation

1. Check for the bubbling and fizzing sound _____

2. Check the temperature of the fermentation room _____

3. Check the specific gravity of the wash:

    1st SG Check: Date _____ SG _____

    2nd SG Check: Date _____ SG _____

    Terminal Gravity: Date _____ TG _____ PA _____

    Net PA _____

Notes:
_____
_____
_____

PEACH MOONSHINE

For this peach moonshine recipe we keep all of the juice and pomace (skin and pulp) together, so it is more of a mash. We will be using a fair amount of water and sugar to help increase the volume of moonshine we produce. You can always make a smaller batch if you wish, just keep the ingredient ratios the same.

Water - 6 gallons
Fresh peaches - 25 lb.
White Sugar - 6 lb.
Pectic Enzyme - 4½ tsp
Fermax yeast nutrient - 9 tsp
Lalvin EC-1118 Champagne yeast - 3½ tsp

COOKING THE MASH

1. SLICE THE PEACHES AND CUT UP INTO SMALL CHUNKS
Cut up the peaches into pieces approximately 2x2" in size. Remove the pit/stone.

2. CRUSH THE FRUIT
You can use a fruit crusher for this.

3. PUT THE CRUSHED PEACHES INTO THE COOKING POT

4. ADD THE WATER
An RV water filter works well for filtering your mash water.

5. COOK ON LOW BOIL FOR 30 MINUTES
Keep the lid on the pot. Stir up the mash every few minutes to help it heat evenly. Cooking the mash will sterilize it and help break down the pulp and produce more fermentable juice.

6. ADD THE SUGAR
Mix in the sugar until dissolved.

7. TAKE A SPECIFIC GRAVITY READING OF THE JUICE

Take a sample of juice from your mash and allow it to cool to room temperature. Use a refractometer or saccharometer to measure the specific gravity of the juice. It should be about 1.080 for a potential alcohol of about 10.5%. Record this data in your worksheet/record. This will be your OG reading.

8. ALLOW THE MASH TO COOL TO 27°C (80°F)

You can let the mash cool naturally - takes a few hours - or use an emersion wort chiller to cool it faster.

9. ADD PECTIC ENZYME

Mix in the pectic enzyme. Make sure your mash temperature is down to about 27°C (80°F) before adding the pectic enzyme. Higher temperatures can decrease the effectiveness of the enzyme. Pectic enzyme will help break down the pectin, especially in the pulp, and produce more juice.

FERMENTATION

Fermentation for fruit mash should be complete in 4 to 6 days. If fermentation stops, stuck fermentation, add another half dose of nutrients, mix it up, and let it continue fermenting until TG, or close to it, is reached.

1. SANITIZE FERMENTATION EQUIPMENT

See chapter 6.

2. SECURE MASH BAG INTO THE FERMENTER

3. CHECK THE WASH TEMPERATURE

Should be 24°C-27°C (75°F-80°F). Adjust if necessary.

4. CHECK THE pH OF THE WASH

The pH of your peach juice wash should be between 4.0-4.5. If it is too low add calcium carbonate to raise it. If it is too high add citric acid to lower it. Add a ½ tsp at a time, mix it in good, and recheck the pH. Keep adding more until the pH is where it should be. See pH in the expanded glossary for more in depth information.

5. ADD THE YEAST NUTRIENTS

Mix in the nutrients. Although apples provide a good deal of nutrients to the yeast, I still recommend using some nutrients to make <u>sure</u> they are well fed. Healthy yeast produce good quality alcohol.

6. PITCH THE YEAST

We are using EC-1118 Champagne yeast for this recipe. Champagne yeast is popular for fermenting fruit juice, but there are other strains of yeast you can also use. Make a yeast starter by getting a cup of 43°C (110°F) water. Add a tsp of sugar. Add the required amount of yeast. Mix it up and let it sit for about 15 minutes. The yeast will hydrate and start becoming active. active. Once you see a couple of inches of barm (foam) on top of the water it is ready to pitch. Make sure the wash has cooled down to about 27°C (80°F). Pour the yeast starter into your fruit wash, mix everything well.

7. AERATE THE WASH

Pour the wash between two 5 gallon buckets 3 times. I fill a bucket about half way with wash, pour it back and forth 3 times, then pour it into the fermenter. You could also use an aquarium pump to aerate - much easier method. The yeast need the oxygen during the lag phase of fermentation - don't skip this step.

8. POUR THE WASH INTO THE FERMENTER

9. PUT THE LID ON THE FERMENTER AND LABEL IT

10. PLACE THE FERMENTER IN YOUR FERMENTATION ROOM

11. SET THE ROOM TEMPERATURE TO 24-27°C (75-80°F)

PROCEDURES DURING FERMENTATION

1. CHECK FOR THE BUBBLING AND FIZZING SOUND

2. MONITOR THE TEMPERATURE OF YOUR FERMENTATION ROOM

3. CHECK THE SG EVERY COUPLE OF DAYS UNTIL THE TG IS REACHED

WORKSHEETS

For recovering the wash through bottling, use the instructions for making Classic Moonshine in chapter 3, pages 56-80. The same procedures can be used for making peach moonshine.

For cooking the mash, fermentation, and procedures during fermentation photocopy and use the worksheets on the next two pages.

For recovering the wash through bottling, photocopy and use the classic moonshine worksheets, pages 84-86, the procedures are the same.

PEACH MOONSHINE
WORKSHEET

Recipe   Batch No. _____   Batch Name_____

Water - 6 gallons

Fresh peaches - 25 lb.

White Sugar - 6 lb.

Pectic Enzyme - 4½ tsp.

Fermax yeast nutrient - 9 tsp

Lalvin EC-1118 Champagne yeast - 3½ tsp

Cooking the Mash

1. **Cut peaches into small chunks _____**   Date _____

2. **Crush and mash the fruit _____**

3. **Put the peach mash into the cooking pot _____**

4. **Add the water _____**

5. **Cook on low boil for 30 minutes _____**

6. **Allow to cool down to about 27°C (80°F) _____**

7. **Add the sugar _____**

8. **Check the specific gravity of the juice OG _____ PA _____**

9. **Add the pectic enzyme _____**

Notes:
_____
_____
_____
_____

Fermentation

Date _____ Time _____

1. Sanitize fermentation equipment _____

2. Secure mash bag in fermenter _____

3. Check to make sure the mash temperature is around 24-27°C (75-80°F) _____

4. Check the juice pH (want 4.0-4.5) _____ Adjusted pH _____

5. Add yeast nutrients, mix _____

6. Pitch yeast, mix _____

7. Aerate the mash _____

8. Pour mash into fermenter _____

9. Put the lid on fermenter and label - Batch number, date, time, OG _____

10. Place fermenter in fermentation room _____

11. Set heater temperature to 24-27°C (75-80°F) _____

Procedures During Fermentation

1. Check for the bubbling and fizzing sound _____

2. Check the temperature of the fermentation room _____

3. Check the specific gravity of the wash:

    1st SG Check: Date _____ SG _____

    2nd SG Check: Date _____ SG _____

    Terminal Gravity: Date _____ TG _____ PA _____

    Net PA _____

Notes:
_____
_____
_____

Chapter 5

How to Create Your Own Moonshine Recipes

Creating your own moonshine recipes is an easy process requiring a few basic calculations. Learning how to design your own recipes allows you to be more creative and use whatever carbohydrate sources you want. Although classic moonshine is made from corn, barley, and sometimes sugar, you can make it from other grains, fruits, vegetable, molasses, honey, or agave syrup. To make your own successful recipes it is critical to calculate the expected amount of fermentable sugar your recipe will produce. You want to have enough sugar to produce a productive fermentation and produce a reasonable amount of alcohol. You don't want a sugar content that is too low because you won't be able to produce enough alcohol to make it worth your time and expense. On the other hand, you don't want too much sugar which can kill your yeast and end a fermentation too soon.

118

HOW TO CALCULATE EXPECTED OG AND PA FOR ANY MOONSHINE GRAIN BILL/RECIPE

Calculating original gravity and potential alcohol makes it possible for you to determine if a particular grain bill/recipe will actually produce an adequate amount of product. There are a few concepts to learn before making these calculations.

Mash Efficiency (ME)

Mash efficiency is also known as Extraction Efficiency. It is simply the amount of starch in the grain, or any other organic material, that is actually converted to fermentable sugars. All grains have specific efficiencies, but we can use an <u>average</u> of 75%. Meaning that about 75% of the starch in our grain will be converted to fermentable sugars; glucose, sucrose, maltose, etc. Knowing this is helpful in determining how much grain, or other starch source, we need to add to a mash to achieve the desired original gravity and potential alcohol level. Knowing how to use extraction efficiency will enable you to develop your own moonshine recipes with the assurance they will work out properly.

Mash efficiency is affected by several factors

Grain Crush - is the grain ground or crushed enough to expose the endosperm which contains the starch.

pH - the pH affects the enzymes that are responsible for saccharification of the starch. 5.2 to 5.8 is the best pH range.

Temperature - proper temperature affects starch conversion.

Grain-to-Water Ratio - the proper amount of water is required to convert starches to sugars. For grains I recommend a 3:1 ratio. Three pounds grain to 1 gallon water.

Water Chemistry - moderately hard water is best for mashing. Hardness refers to the amount of calcium and magnesium in the water. These minerals can be added if necessary.

When you put together a mash bill, or recipe, for any kind of mash, you can use the specific gravity values for each ingredient plus the 75% average mash efficiency value to determine the total _estimated_ original gravity of your wort. That information will allow you to create recipes that meet your target original gravity and potential alcohol goals.

Specific Gravity for Grains and Sugars Table, Appendix pg. 147.

This table show the specific gravity for common grains and sugar sources used to make moonshine. You will need to look up the SG for each item you are using in a grain bill/recipe.

Fruit Juice Specific Gravity Table, Appendix, pg. 150.

This table show the specific gravity for common fruits that can be used to make moonshine. You will need to look up the SG for each item you are using in a recipe.

Calculating Expected Original Gravity and Potential Alcohol

For an example, we will use the grain bill for classic moonshine.

8 Gallons water

Corn Meal - 85%, 20.4 lb.

Barley Malt - 15%, 3.6 lb.

Total Mash Volume: 10 Gallons

The following values are the specific gravity (SG) of 1 pound of grain added to 1 gallon of water. Specific gravity values are from the Specific Gravity for Grains and Sugars table in the appendix, page 147. A mash efficiency of 75% is used.

Corn meal 1.037 (37 gravity points).....................20.4 X 37 = 754.8

Barley Malt   1.037 (37 gravity points)...................3.6 X 37 = <u>133.2</u>

$$888$$

888 X .75 (ME) = 666 total gravity points

666/10 gal. mash volume = 66.6 = 1.067 Expected OG, PA = about 8.8% (Good to go)

Our expected OG and PA is within out desired range.

You can use this process to check the expected OG and PA for any grain bill or recipe you create. Make sure your recipes will work before you start them; adjust them if necessary.

ADDING SUGAR TO A MASH

If you create a grain bill or recipe that ends up with an expected SG and PA lower than you want you can add some sugar to boost it. You don't want to go overboard when adding sugar however. Too much sugar will reduce the flavor of your moonshine and can have harmful affects on your yeast. I recommend shooting for a SG of 1.080 which is a PA of 10.5%; between 8 and 12% PA is good. Follow the instructions below when adding sugar. Refer to the Sugar Required for Target Specific Gravity and Potential Alcohol table in the appendix, page 149.

Let's say you create a 10 gallon moonshine mash and your expected OG is 1.050 for a PA of 6.6%, but you want a PA of about 10%. Calculate the required sugar as follows: from the table on page 149.

OG of 1.050 equates to 21 ounces of sugar per gallon of mash.

Desired OG of 1.080 (10.5% PA) equates to 33 ounces of sugar per gallon of mash.

33 - 21 = 12 ounces per gallon of mash needed.

12 X 10 gal. mash = 120 ounces (7.5 pounds) of sugar needed.

Add 7.5 pounds of sugar, mix it in, recheck your gravity.

Chapter 6

Cleaning and Sanitizing Equipment

Sanitation is obviously important when cooking and fermenting. This chapter includes some sanitation products to use and some tips on keeping your equipment clean.

SANITIZING A STAINLESS STEEL STILL AND OTHER NON-COPPER EQUIPMENT

Bleach

Use about 1 tbsp of bleach per gallon of water for cleaning/sanitizing your non-copper equipment. Do not use bleach on cooper items, it will corrode the metal. Use a bleach solution for your stainless steel still, mash cooking pot, five gallon buckets, fermenter and lid, mixing paddle, jars and plastic bowl. Just wipe down the items with the bleach solution and triple rinse. Rinsing three times is a good practice to make sure all of the bleach solution is removed from the item being cleaned. You should sanitize all equipment before each new batch.

122

CLEANING A COPPER STILL AND OTHER COPPER EQUIPMENT

White Vinegar

Use white vinegar and water to clean your still, condenser and alcohol parrot. It is a good cleaner, but does not sanitize. In realty, your copper still gets sanitized every time you heat it while distilling.

Outside of Still

Mix 1 tbsp of salt, 1 cup white vinegar and enough flour to make a paste.

Apply to the outside of your still.

Let it sit for 30 minutes.

Wash off with cloth and water.

Inside of Still - Light Cleaning

A light cleaning is all that is necessary most of the time.

Put about 1 gallon of water and 2 cups of vinegar into your still.

Scrub out the still with a scrubber pad or brush.

Triple rinse. Do a light cleaning before each new batch.

Inside of Still- Thorough Cleaning

After every 10 distillation runs I recommend a thorough cleaning. Put 2 gallons of water and 2 gallons of vinegar into your still. Put the still head on, connect your condenser and run the still. Heat the solution up to boiling and let it run through your system for 10 minutes. Don't forget to set up a collection jar or you'll have hot vinegar water all over the floor. Triple rinse.

STAR SAN

Star San is an acid-based no-rinse sanitizer that is effective and easy to use. It is made from food-grade phosphoric acid, safe for people and the environment. Star San is self-foaming which helps it to penetrate cracks and crevices. It is odorless and flavorless, and does not require rinsing when used at the recommended dilution. Use only 1 oz Star San per 5 gallons of water and just 1 to 2 minutes of contact time. Used as a soaking solution, it can also be applied by hand (wear gloves) or with a spray bottle. It is also reusable. A solution of Star San will remain effective for up to three to four weeks in a sealed container; it is effective as long as the pH is 3 or lower.

PBW

PBW (Powdered Brewery Wash) is a patented alkali cleaner originally developed for Coors, now widely used in commercial breweries across North America. Use 1 to 2 Use 1 to 2 ounces per gallon for cleaning kettles, 3/4 ounce per gallon for fermenters, kegs, tanks, and other equipment. Soak equipment overnight in PBW solution; rinse the following morning - no scrubbing required!

Distilling Safety

Distilling spirits is actually very safe if common sense is applied.

Here are some of the critical items to keep in mind when distilling.

1. DO NOT LEAVE YOUR STILL UNATTENDED.

2. AN ELECTRIC HOT PLATE IS THE SAFEST WAY TO HEAT YOUR STILL.

3. A PROPANE BURNER CAN BE USED WITH PROPER PRECAUTIONS.

4. KEEP YOUR CONDENSER WATER COOL.

5. HIGH PROOF ALCOHOL AND VAPOR ARE VERY FLAMMABLE.

6. DO NOT FILL YOUR STILL MORE THAN 3/4 FULL.

7. DISCARD THE FORESHOTS - THEY CONTAIN METHANOL.

8. KEEP A FIRE EXTINGUISHER NEARBY.

9. SEAL ALL LEAKS IN YOUR SYSTEM WITH FLOUR PASTE.

10. MAKE SURE TO HAVE GOOD VENTILATION.

11. USE GLASS DISTILLATE COLLECTION JARS - NEVER PLASTIC.

12. DIRECT THE DISTILLATE AWAY FROM YOUR STILL.

Expanded Glossary

Adjuncts

Unmalted grains added to the mash.

Aerate

To introduce air and oxygen into something. Introducing air into the wort, for example.

Alcohols and other Compounds in the Distillate

There are a number of different alcohols and compounds produced by the yeast during fermentation. When we distill the wash the different alcohols and compounds will boil and vaporize at different temperatures. The table below shows the different products that may be distilled out of a typical wash and the temperature at which each will boil. These are the temperatures at which each product will boil if the solution is made of 100% of that particular product. For example, if we had a container with 100% pure ethanol in it, it would boil and 78.4°C. When we have a typical wash containing different fractions of each product, the actual boiling points will be higher due to the fact that they are not in a 100% pure state; they are diluted in water. The boiling points are used as a guide to help determine when each product is vaporized during distillation.

Product	Formula	Temp.
Acetaldehyde	C_2H_4O	20.2°C (68.4°F)
Ethyl Formate	$C_3H_6O_2$	54.3°C (129.7°F)
Acetone	C_3H_6O	56.0°C (132.8°F)
Methanol - Wood Alcohol	CH_3OH	64.7°C (148.5°F)
Ethyl Acetate	$C_4H_8O_2$	77.1°C (170.8°F)
Ethanol	C_2H_6O	78.4°C (173.1°F)
2-Propanol	C_3H_8O	82.6°C (180.7°F)
1-Propanol - Rubbing alcohol	C_3H_8O	97.0°C (206.6°F)
Water	H_2O	100.0°C (212°F)
Butanol	$C_4H_{10}O$	117.7°C (243.9°F)
Acetic Acid	CH_3COOH	118.1°C (244.6°F)
Amyl Alcohol	$C_5H_{12}O$	131.6°C (268.9°F)
Furfural	$C_5H_4O_2$	161.7°C (323.1°F)

126

Alcohol By Volume (ABV)

Alcohol By Volume is usually abbreviated as ABV. It is the concentration of total alcohol, as a percentage, in the distillate or in a bottle of spirits.
For example, 40% ABV.

Alpha-Amylase Enzyme

Alpha-amylase enzyme is an enzyme produced by germinating seeds or grain like barley. The enzyme helps break down long chained sugars (starch) into smaller carbohydrates containing one, two, or three glucose molecules. These can then be fermented by the yeast. The picture below illustrates the structure of a starch molecule. The enzyme breaks the bonds in between the glucose molecules.

Alcohol Hydrometer (Alcoholometer)

Hydrometer used to measure the alcohol content of a solution. The tool shows the alcohol by volume (abv), as a percentage, as well as the proof of the solution. Proof is two times the abv.

Alcohol Parrot

A copper tube that receives distillate from a still condenser and holds an alcohol hydrometer. This allows the distiller to see real-time abv readings as the distillation proceeds.

Amylopectin

A water-insoluble polysaccharide and highly branched polymer of α-glucose units found in plants. It is one of the two components of starch, the other being amylose.

Amylose

Amylose is a polysaccharide made of α-D-glucose units bonded to each other through α glycosidic bonds. Amylose is a straight linear chain of glucose molecules linked by α-1,4 glycosidic linkages It is one of the two components of starch, making up approximately 20-30%.

Angel's Share

The spirit lost to evaporation out of the oak barrels during aging. About 2% of the spirits are lost to evaporation each year.

Attenuation

The decline in the specific gravity of the wort as the yeast converts sugars to alcohol. Can also be expressed as the percentage of sugars the yeast consumes during fermentation, normally from 65 to 80%.

Auto Siphon

A convenient tool for removing wash from a fermenter and backset from a still.

Back Set

The wash left at the end of a stripping run that can be added into the next batch of mash. Normally used to replace 25% of the water needed in a new batch of mash. This creates a sour mash and acidifies (lowers the pH) the mash.

Bacteria

Bacteria are microscopic single-celled organisms. There are many kinds of bacteria, some are harmful, but many are beneficial. There are several species of Lactobacillus bacteria that can enter your mash naturally or can be added intentionally. Lactobacillus will produce various acids that are used in the creation of esters in the wort. The esters will have a flavorful effect on your whiskey. You can purchase Lactobacillus bacteria to incorporate into your mash if desired.

Baking Soda

Sodium bicarbonate, $NaHCO_3$. Used to raise pH.

Barm

The foam formed on the top of a fermenting liquid or mash.

Base Malt

Base malts make up part of the grist in an all-grain mash. If you are making a bourbon for example, barley malt would be the base malt to which other grains are added.

Beta-Amylase Enzyme

Beta-amylase is an enzyme also produced by germinating seeds or grains. The enzyme breaks chemical bonds at the end of the sugar chains (starch). This process produces two-chained sugars like maltose. It is an important process in whiskey making because is helps facilitate the saccharification process.

Blending

The process of carefully adding heads and or tails to a batch of hearts in order to attain a certain flavor in the final whiskey product. This takes a fair amount of skill to do correctly.

Boiling

Heating a liquid to the temperature at which it bubbles and turns to vapor. Boiling occurs below the surface of a heated liquid. Ethanol boils in relation to its concentration in water. The lower the concentration of ethanol in water, the higher the boiling temperature of the ethanol.

Bottled in Bond

Bottled in bond is a label for an American-made distilled beverage that has been aged and bottled according to a set of legal regulations contained in the United States government's Standards of Identity for Distilled Spirits, as originally laid out in the Bottled-in-Bond Act of 1897.

Carbohydrate

The main types of carbohydrates are monosaccharides, disaccharides, and polysaccharides. Carbohydrates consist of molecules of glucose bonded together. Glucose molecules are composed of carbon, hydrogen, and oxygen atoms in the chemical structure of $C_6H_{12}O_6$. Glucose is also known as a simple sugar or monosaccharide. It is the primary source of energy for living things including the yeast we rely on for fermentation.

Charge

The charge is the amount of liquid, e.g., low wines, being placed in a still for distillation.

Citric Acid, $HOC(CH_2CO_2H)_2$

Citric acid is an organic compound. It is a colorless weak organic acid. It occurs naturally in citrus fruits. Citric acid can be used to increase the acidity of a mash. Many of the enzymes that break down the starches in a mash function best at lower pH levels. Using citric acid can help lower the mash pH level to increase the starch conversion rate.

Congeners

Congeners are substances other than ethanol that are produced during fermentation. They can effect the flavor of the distillate positively or negatively.

Copper Sulfate (CuSO$_4$)

When distilling with a copper still, sulfur, produced by the yeast during fermentation, binds with the copper to produce copper sulfate. This is good because it removes the sulfur from your distillate. When you clean your still the copper sulfate is washed away.

Cuts

During distillation the cuts are the points at which the distiller separates the heads and the tails leaving the hearts of the run.

Cutting

Diluting an alcohol spirit by adding water. Also known as proofing down.

DADY (Distiller's Active Dry Yeast)

DADY is a good all-purpose yeast that is good for making whiskey and other spirits.

Dephlegmator (duh-fleg-mater)

Also known as a reflux condenser, a dephlegmator is located at the top of a column still. Its purpose is to condense vapors back into liquid and send them back down the column into the still where they are re-vaporized (reflux). This creates a purer distillate.

Dextrin

A type of starch made from mixtures of polymers of D-glucose molecules. Produced by breaking apart starch or glycogen.

Dextrinase

An enzyme in malted grain that cleaves the alpha-1,6 linkage in dextrins to produce glucose.

Diacetyl (CH$_3$CO)$_2$

A yellow or green liquid with an intensely buttery flavor. Diacetyl is a by-product produced by yeast during fermentation and occurs naturally in alcoholic beverages.

Diammonium Phosphate (DAP)

DAP is a pure form of yeast nutrient containing nitrogen and phosphorus. Use ½ tsp per 5 gallons of mash. Not needed in all grain mashes.

Distillate

The liquid produced from the process of distillation. In our case, ethanol plus other forms of alcohol.

Enzyme

A protein that acts as a biological catalyst. Catalysts accelerate chemical reactions. Acts upon a substrate and produces a product.

Enzyme Conversion

Enzymes are compounds responsible for converting starches in a mash into fermentable sugars.

Esters

Esters are compounds produced during fermentation. They result from the combination of alcohols and fatty acids or acetates. Esters add aromas and flavors to the spirit.

Important Esters in Distilling	Flavor
Butyl Acetate	Apple
Ethyl Acetate	Pear
Ethyl Butyrate	Pineapple
Ethyl Cinnamate	Cinnamon
Ethyl Hexanoate	Apple
Isoamyl Acetate	Banana
Methyl Trans-Cinnamate	Strawberry
Octyl Acetate	Orange
Propyl Acetate	Pear

Esterification

A reaction of an alcohol with an acid to produce an ester and water.

Ethanol (C_2H_5OH)

Ethanol, also known as ethyl alcohol, is one of the alcohols produced by yeast during sugar fermentation. It has a specific gravity of 0.789, less dense and lighter than water.

Evaporation

Evaporation occurs at the surface of a boiling liquid as the liquid transitions into vapor.

Exogenous Enzyme

Enzymes that are supplied from an external source, not naturally found in the grains or other carbohydrate sources being mashed.

Extraction Efficiency

AKA Mash Efficiency. The amount of fermentable sugar actually produced from a mash. An average mash efficiency for grains is 75%.

FAN (Free Amino Nitrogen)

The concentration of individual amino acids and small peptides (one to three units) which can be utilized by yeast for cell growth and reproduction during fermentation. |

Feints

The final distillate from a spirit run. The feints are low in alcohol and can be added to the next run and redistilled.

Felting

Felting is a condition where the grain roots grow together during the malting process. It is not a desirable situation. It makes it had to separate the grains before drying and further processing.

Fermentation

Fermentation is the process of converting sugars, like glucose and maltose, into acids, carbon dioxide (CO_2), and various alcohols by yeasts. The breakdown of glucose also releases carbon atoms which can be used by the yeast to grow and reproduce (budding). It is important to make sure the yeasts have an ample supply of oxygen and other nutrients at the beginning of their life cycle for efficient fermentation.

Fermenter

AKA Fermentation bucket, a fermenter is a container that wort or wash is poured or siphoned into after cooling to facilitate fermentation.

Ferment Off The Grain

The wort is separated from the mash and fermented.

Ferment On The Grain

The entire mash, including grains and wort, is fermented.

Flocculation

Yeasts' ability to clump together and settle out at the end of a fermentation. They are dormant at this stage, not dead.

Foreshots

The first few ounces of distillate produced during a distillation. They contain methanol and other volatile alcohols.

Fructose ($C_6H_{12}O_6$)

Fructose (Frook - tose) is a simple sugar that is a polymer of glucose. It has the exact same chemical formula as glucose, just arranged differently.

Fructophilic

Prefers to ferment fructose. Some yeast strains will ferment fructose first, then glucose. They are fructophilic.

Fusel Oils

Fusel oils are higher order alcohols. Fusel is a German word which means "bad liquor." They have an oily consistency, smell like a wet dog, and taste bad. Fusel oils include: propanol, butanol, amyl alcohol, and furfural.

Gelatinization

When using corn meal or polenta as your source of corn in a batch, the corn must first be gelatinized. This involves heating the corn in water which breaks the bonds between the starch molecules. This basically dissolves the starch and allows the corn to absorb more water. The mixture will become very thick. Once the corn is gelatinized you can add the remaining grains (e.g., barley malt, rye) and proceed to cook the batch.

Glucoamylase

Glucoamylase is a fungal-derived enzyme which breaks down dextrins into simple sugars.

Glucose ($C_6H_{12}O_6$)

A simple sugar which is an important energy source in living organisms and is a component of many carbohydrates.

Glucophilic

Prefers to ferment glucose. Some yeast strains prefer to ferment glucose first. They are glucophilic.

Glycogen ($C_{24}H_{42}O_{21}$)

Glycogen is a multibranched polysaccharide of glucose that serves as a form of energy storage in animals, fungi, and bacteria. The polysaccharide structure represents the main storage form of glucose in the body.

Glycolysis

The breakdown of glucose by enzymes, releasing energy and pyruvic acid.

Grain Bill

In the distilling industry the grain bill is simply a list of which grains are used to make the mash and the percentage of each. For example, the grain bill for Jack Daniels Tennessee Whiskey is 80% corn, 12% rye and 8% malted barley. Of course, trying to make Jack Daniels whiskey isn't just a matter of using their grain bill. They use various techniques in their production process that produces the unique flavors of Jack Daniels, techniques that are closely guarded secrets.

Grain Cap

The layer of grain pushed up by carbon dioxide produced by yeast during fermentation. You will see a grain cap form at the top of your fermenter.

Gravity

Refers to specific gravity. The total amount of dissolved solids in water; usually referring to dissolved sugars.

Gravity Unit

Specific gravity of different mash ingredients can be shown as gravity units. For example, the specific gravity of one pound of flaked corn in one gallon of water is 1.037. This would be 37 gravity units. It is usually expressed as the **PPG (Points Per Pound Per Gallon).** Gravity units are used to calculate the total original gravity (OG) of a mash or wort.

Grist

Ground grain.

Gypsum

Calcium sulfate, $CaSO_4$. Used to lower pH.

Heads

The first major part of the distillate is called the heads. The heads contain compounds like acetone, acetaldehyde, acetate and some ethanol. They have a strong, almost fruity smell and taste harsh. Heads can be discarded or collected and added to the next spirit run. Approximately 20-30% of the liquid collected during a distillation run will be heads.

Hearts

The hearts contain mainly ethanol and are the part of the spirit run we want to collect and make into whiskey. Hearts will have a light sweet smell and a light sweet, smooth taste. The skill of the distiller is in developing the ability to smell and taste the different fractions of distillate in order to separate the heads, hearts and tails effectively. Approximately 30-40% of the run will be hearts. See Appendix A for an illustration of Heads, Hearts and Tails.

Hydrolysis

Hydrolysis is any chemical reaction in which a molecule of water breaks one or more chemical bonds causing a larger molecule to be broken into smaller molecules.

Infusion Mash

A mashing technique where hot brewing water is blended with malts to create a mash that only has one rest, at saccharification temperature.

Iodine Starch Test

Used to test for the presence of starch in a solution. Place a few drops of wort on a plate. Place a few drops of iodine into the wort and mix together. If it turns blue/black there is still starch that has not been converted to fermentable sugars.

Krausen

Foamy head that forms on top of fermenting wort after about 4 hours of fermentation. Consists of dead yeast and proteins.

Lactic Acid ($C_3H_6O_3$)

Lactic acid is an organic acid. It can be used to reduce alkalinity (lower pH) in mash. The lactic acid used is food grade and made by fermentation of natural beet or cane sugar.

Lautering

To rinse off and separate the wort from the mash. Lauter comes from the German word abläutern, meaning to rinse off or purify.

Lees

The layer of dormant yeast that accumulate in the bottom of the fermenter or vat.

Liebig Condenser

A Liebig condenser is a straight condenser consisting of a single tube within a larger tube or water jacket. It is used to cool and condense a gas/vapor back to a liquid. It is often used as a primary condenser for distilling alcoholic spirits.

Lime

Calcium carbonate, $CaCO_3$. Used to raise pH.

Liquefaction

Breaking down gelatinized starch molecules by alpha-amylase enzyme.

Low Wines

The distillate produced from the first distillation (stripping run) of a fermented wash. Usually have an abv of about 40%.

Lyne Arm

The tube going from the still head to the condenser.

Malt

Any germinated cereal grain that has been dried with hot air in order to halt germination. Known as "malting."

Malt Extract

A sweet, treacle like syrup, made from malted barley. Used in brewing.

Maceration

To soften and break down organic tissue, e.g., fruits, by exposure to moisture.

Maltase

An enzyme in barley that hydrolyzes (breaks down) maltose into glucose.

Maltose

Maltose, also known as maltobiose or malt sugar, is a disaccharide formed from two units of glucose joined with an alpha bond.

Mash

Cooked mixture of grains and water.

Mash Bill

The mix of grains being used to make a spirit.

Mashing

The process of extracting starches from grains with water and enzymatically converting them into fermentable sugars yeast can use.

Mash Bag

A net-like bag used to cook or ferment mash in. The bag makes it easy to remove the grain and separate out the wort from the mash.

Mash Efficiency

AKA Extraction Efficiency. The amount of fermentable sugar actually produced from the starches in a mash. An average mash efficiency for grains is 75%.

Mash Tun
A vessel used for mixing ground grains (grist) with temperature-controlled water.

Neutral Based Spirit
Non-flavored alcohol of 95% abv obtained chiefly from grain or molasses.

Miscible
Liquids that can form a homogeneous mixture when added together.

New Make Spirit
New make is unaged whiskey. The clear liquid that comes off the still at about 70% abv and before it's moved into a barrel. It is most commonly associated with Scotch, but new make can be any style of whiskey.

Open Fermentation
Fermentations that take place in vessels that are open to the environment.

Original Gravity (OG)
The starting specific gravity of a wort before fermentation indicating the amount of sugar present. Can be used to determine the potential alcohol of the wort.

Oxidation
Oxidation occurs when an atom, molecule, or ion loses one or more electrons in a chemical reaction. Oxidation doesn't necessarily involve oxygen, but sometimes it does. Originally, the term was used when oxygen caused electron loss in a reaction.

Pasteurization
Pasteurization is the process of heating, juice, wine, beer, and other liquid foods to kill yeast, bacteria, and other pathogens. Heat to 71°C (160°F) for 1 minute.

pH

Potential of hydrogen. pH measures the acidity and alkalinity of a substance. We are concerned about the pH of our mash and our wort prior to fermentation. The pH scale is a logarithmic scale that goes from 0 to 14. Seven is neutral, anything below 7 is acidic, and anything above 7 is alkaline. Acidic substances have a high concentration of hydrogen ions (H^+) and alkaline substances have a high concentration of hydroxyl ions (OH^-).

In the distilling business the optimum pH for mash is between 5.2 and 5.7, moderately acidic. This pH range improves the activity of the enzymes responsible for saccharification and gives us a better conversion of the starches in the mash to glucose. It is a good idea to check the pH of your mash with a pH test strip or a digital pH meter. The good news is that mash is naturally in the pH range of 5.2 to 5.7 because grains are acidic by nature.

The optimum pH for fermentation by the yeast is between 4.0 and 4.5. Yeast thrive in a acidic environment and are the most healthy in this pH range. This pH also helps control bacterial growth.

You should check the pH of your wort prior to fermentation. If the pH values for either your mash of your wort are high or low you can adjust them quiet easily. For a pH that is too low, too acidic, you can add calcium carbonate (lime). Mix in 1/2 tsp at a time. Recheck your pH. Keep adding 1/2 tsp at a time until you get it into the correct range. For a pH that is to high, too alkaline, add citric acid or calcium sulfate (gypsum). Mix in 1/2 tsp at a time. Recheck your pH. Keep adding 1/2 tsp at a time until you get it into the correct range. When you check your pH levels you might find they are fine. However, there are variables that can cause your pH to be out of the correct range, one of which is your water.

Pitching Yeast

Putting yeast into the mash or the wort.

Polishing

Filtering the distillate to remove congeners. An activated carbon filter is normally used. Also removes flavor.

PPG

Points Per Pound Per Gallon. The number of specific gravity points per pound of ingredient in a gallon of water. For example, a specific gravity of 1.080 would be 80 gravity points.

Polysaccharide

Polysaccharides, or polycarbohydrates, are the most abundant carbohydrates found in food, including grains. They are long chain polymeric carbohydrates composed of monosaccharide units, like glucose, bound together by glycosidic linkages. Often referred to as complex carbohydrates, polysaccharides can react with water using amylase enzymes as a catalyst, which breaks the polysaccharides apart to yield individual glucose molecules.

Potential Alcohol (PA)

This is the amount of alcohol we would expect to be produced from the fermentation of the wort. Most batches of wort will have between 8 and 10% potential alcohol.

Proof

Alcohol proof is twice the percentage of alcohol by volume. So if you have a whiskey that is 40% abv it would be 80 proof.

Primary Condenser

A primary condenser is the main condenser being used during a distillation. The condenser cools alcohol vapors back into liquid as the vapors pass through the condenser. A pot still setup typically used a worm condenser, where a column still uses a shell and tube condenser.

Protease

An enzyme that breaks down proteins into amino acids.

Racking

Moving wash from one vessel to another.

Rectification

The process of repeated distillation that produces a purified product. The product being ethanol in the case of spirit distillation.

Saccharification

The breaking apart of polysaccharides (complex sugars and starches) to soluble sugars like glucose is called saccharification. Malted barley containing beta-amylase enzyme, and the addition of alpha-amylase enzyme to the mash, break the starch molecules in the grains apart to produce single molecules of glucose (simple sugar). The glucose can then be consumed by the yeast during fermentation.

Shotgun Condenser

A shotgun condenser is a type of primary condenser that has multiple tubes, usually from 3 to 7, inside a main outer tube. Whereas a Liebig condenser has a single tube within the main outer tube.

Single Barrel

Single barrel whiskey (or single cask whisky), is whiskey that comes from an individual aging barrel, instead of being created by blending together the contents of different barrels.

Single Malt Scotch

Single malt whisky made at a single distillery in Scotland.

Small Batch Whiskey

Small batch whiskey is whiskey that is produced by mixing the contents of a small number of selected barrels. So, it is blended whiskey.

Soluble

A substance able to be dissolved, especially in water.

Sour Mash

Sour mash whiskey is made by adding some backset or spent mash from a previous batch to the mash of a new batch. Sour mash is typically made with backset contributing 25% of the total liquid in a mash. In the case of using spent mash, about 5 pounds is added to a 10 gallon mash. The mash becomes "sour" from the growth of Lactobacillus bacteria. The bacteria produces lactic acid which lowers the pH of the mash, known as acidification. This keeps other bacteria from growing in, and ruining, the mash. Ensuring the proper mash pH helps to control bacteria like Clostridium butyricum which can ruin the batch. The use of sour mash can create a fuller flavor profile in the finished product and help maintain a more consistent flavor between batches.

Sparging

Sparging is a step at the end of the mashing process where hot water, 170°F (77°C), is run through the grain bed to extract more of the sugar from the grain.

Specific Gravity (SG)

In technical terms, the density of a substance divided by the density of the water. In distilling, the substance would be sugar or alcohol. For example, 1 gallon of pure water has a SG of 1.000, adding a pound of cane sugar increases the SG to 1.046.

Specialty Malt

Specialty malts are malted grains that vary based on processing and grain type. They undergo the same malting processes as other malts but have experienced different heat and moisture treatments designed to produce different flavor and color. Roasting is a common treatment.

Spelt (Triticum spelta)

Spelt is an ancient species of wheat that was cultivated as far back as 5000 BC. The grain is still grown in some countries.

Spirit

From Aristotle, in 327 B.C., who thought drinking distilled beer or wine put spirit into the body of the drinker.

Starch

AKA amylum. Starch is a polymeric (consisting of many units bonded together) carbohydrate consisting of numerous glucose units joined by glycosidic bonds. This polysaccharide (complex sugar) is produced by most green plants for energy storage. The two main components of starch are amylose (10-20%), and amylopectin (80-90%).

Sugar Hydrometer (Saccharometer)

Hydrometer that measures the specific gravity of a solution; the wort and/or wash in the case of whiskey production. This shows the amount of sugar in the solution which can be used to indicate the potential alcohol.

Tails

The tails occur at the end of the run. Tails do contain some ethanol as well as fusel oils like propanol, butanol and amyl alcohol. Tails also contain water, carbohydrates and proteins. You will know when the tails start because they smell like a wet dog and taste muddy. You will also see an oily sheen on top of the distillate as the tails continue to distill and the distillate will start to look cloudy. Tails can be discarded or collected and added to the next spirit run. Tails will make up approximately 20-30% of a spirit run.

Terminal Gravity (TG)

Also called final gravity, terminal gravity is the specific gravity of a wort or a wash at the end of fermentation. Ideally about 1.000.

Torrified

A process of treating wheat with a high-temperature heat treatment that breaks down the cellular structure of the grain. The torrefied wheat is now pre-gelatinized, so you just need to crush or flake it before adding it to the mash. Produces a wheat that adds a neutral flavor to alcoholic beverages.

Trub

Pronounced "troob", it is the sediment at the bottom of the fermenter that comprises all the un-fermentable products in wort such as fats, proteins, dormant and dead yeast. The yeast layer is known separately as the lees and is part of the trub.

Volatile

A substance that quickly and easily evaporates at normal temperatures.

Vorlauf

A German word for recirculation. The process of pouring heated wort back into the grain bed for sparging.

Wash

The wash is the liquid produced after fermentation is completed. It will normally contain 8 to 10% alcohol. The wash goes into the still for distillation. Wash also refers to the liquid prepared from juice or sugar based products which will be fermented and distilled.

White Dog

The alcohol that comes out of the still and is placed into aging barrels is called white dog. It has no color and little whiskey flavor at this point. It is the raw distillate. White dog is similar to vodka except that it is made only from grains and is distilled at a lower proof than vodka.

Wort

The wort is the liquid produced from the mashing process. It contains glucose which will be fermented by yeast. By using a sugar hydrometer we can measure the specific gravity of the wort and determine what is known as the potential alcohol level.

Wort Chiller

A device made of copper or stainless steel tubing used to cool wort prior to fermentation. The tube is placed into a container of heated wort. A cold water source is connected to the tube. Water flows through the tube and cools the wort.

YAN

Yeast Assimilable Nitrogen. Nitrogen sources that can be used by yeast. Including Free ammonia nitrogen, Ammonia (NH_3), and Ammonium (NH_4).

Yeast

Yeasts are microorganisms that ferment the wort and create alcohol. They are single celled microorganisms classified as members of the fungi kingdom. Saccharomyces cerevisiae is the primary species of yeast used in the distillation of spirits, however, there are many strains of yeast used within that species by the different distilleries. I recommend Distiller's Active Dry Yeast (DADY). This is a good all purpose yeast for distilling that works very well. Once you become an experienced distiller you can branch out and try different strains. Adding yeast to the mash is called "pitching" the yeast. Keep your yeast in an airtight container in the refrigerator.

Yeast Autolysis

Yeast autolysis is the breaking open or rupturing of the yeast cell and the transfer (leaking out) of undesirable substances and off-flavors into the wash. Yeast autolysis is caused by any conditions that stress the yeast during fermentation.

Yeast Energizer

Yeast energizers contain components such as diammonium phosphate, yeast hulls, magnesium sulfate, vitamin B complexes and tricalcium phosphate. Energizers are used to give a boost to a fermentation that is sluggish or stuck during the fermentation process.

Yeast Nutrients

The source of energy consumed by yeast is glucose, but yeast also requires other nutrients in order to reproduce and grow. Yeast nutrient blends contain a mix of trace elements, inorganic nitrogen, organic nitrogen, zinc and phosphates that helps yeast grow and complete fermentation. Yeast nutrients are added to the mash at the same time as the yeast is pitched.

Yeast Starter

To make a yeast starter get a cup of warm water, 43°C (110°F), add 1 tsp of sugar. Mix in the required amount of yeast. Allow it to sit for about 15 minutes, or until you see a good head of foam (barm) forming on top. Then add it to your mash. This rehydrates the yeast and gets it going well before you pitch it. It is a good way to make sure your have viable yeast.

Yogurt

Some distillers use plain yogurt or other sources of Lactobacillus bacteria in their mash recipes. It is believed that Lactobacillus will produce various acids that will be made into esters by the yeast during fermentation. These esters have a positive impact on the flavor of the spirits. Lactobacillus will also help keep bad bacteria from growing in your mash. You can experiment with this.

Appendix Tables

Specific Gravity for Grains and Sugars

ITEM	SPECIFIC GRAVITY
Barley	1.040
Barley Malt - 2 row	1.037
Barley – Flaked	1.032
Barley – Peated	1.034
Barley – Raw	1.028
Chocolate Barley Malt	1.028
Corn - Cracked Feed Corn	1.030
Corn – Flaked	1.037
Corn – Meal	1.037
Honey	1.032
Maple syrup	1.030
Molasses	1.036
Oats – Flaked	1.037
Oats – Rolled	1.025
Rice – Flaked	1.032
Rye – Flaked	1.036
Rye - Malt	1.035
Sugar – Sucrose	1.046
Wheat – Flaked	1.035
Wheat – Malt	1.038
Wheat – Red	1.029
Wheat – White	1.030
Wheat – White malt	1.040

Note: Gravity values for 1 pound of each item added to 1 gal. water.

Average Juice Yield for Fruits

FRUIT	OUNCES PER POUND
Apples	8
Cherries	6
Cranberries	4
Grapes	8
Melons	6
Papayas	3
Peaches	3
Pineapples	4
Plums	8
Strawberries	4
Raspberries	4
Watermelon	8
1 Apple	1/3 Cup Juice
1 Pound Apples	1 Cup Juice
16 Pounds Apples	1 Gallon Juice
48 Apples	1 Gallon Juice

Apple Type and Juice Output
Honeycrisp   Very high   Gala   Medium
Ambrosia   Very high   Egremont Russet   Low
Granny Smith   High
Fuji   Medium high
McIntosh   Medium high
Red delicious   Medium

Sugar Required for Target SG and PA

Use this table when adding sugar to a mash. Adding sugar will increase the potential alcohol of a mash. A good range for PA is from 8 to 12%.

SPECIFIC GRAVITY (SG)	POTENTIAL AL-COHOL (PA%)	AMOUNT OF SUGAR/GAL WASH
1.010	1.3	2 oz.
1.015	1.9	4 oz.
1.020	2.6	7 oz.
1.025	3.3	9 oz.
1.030	3.9	12 oz.
1.035	4.6	15 oz.
1.040	5.2	17 oz.
1.045	5.9	19 oz.
1.050	6.6	21 oz.
1.055	7.2	23 oz.
1.060	7.9	25 oz.
1.065	8.5	27 oz.
1.070	9.2	29 oz.
1.075	9.9	31 oz.
1.080	10.5	33 oz.
1.085	11.2	36 oz.
1.090	11.8	38 oz.
1.095	12.5	40 oz.
1.100	13.2	42 oz.
1.105	13.8	44 oz.
1.110	14.5	46 oz.
1.115	15.1	48 oz.
1.120	15.8	50 oz.
1.125	16.5	52 oz.
1.130	17.1	54 oz.

Fruit Juice - Brix and Specific Gravity

FRUIT	BRIX	SPECIFIC GRAVITY
Apple	4-6 (12)	1.014-1.067 (1.050)
Apricot	4-11 (9)	1.014-1.043 (1.035)
Blackberry	5-10 (6.5)	1.021-1.039 (1.026)
Blueberry	5-12 (7)	1.020-1.051 (1.027)
Cherry	9-19 (15)	1.047-1.080 (1.064)
Cranberry	3-5 (4)	1.012-1.018 (1.016)
Elderberry	7-11 (6)	1.030-1.046
Grape	15-25 (16)	1.060-1.106 (1.065)
Guava	7-11 (9)	1.026-1.047 (1.036)
Honeydew	10	1.039
Lime	0-14 (1)	1.000-1.058 (1.001)
Loganberry	(9)	(1.035)
Mango	11-21 (17)	1.045-1.09 (1.073)
Nectarine	6-12 (9)	1.022-1.047 (1.035)
Orange	2-7(11)	1.007-1.026 (1.043)
Papaya	8	1.031
Passionfruit	5-21 (13)	1.018-1.091 (1.057)
Peach	6-12 (9)	1.022-1.047 (1.035)
Pear	7-13 (10)	1.026-1.052 (1.039)
Pineapple	13	1.052
Plum	11	1.043
Raspberry	7	1.026
Strawberry	3-10 (7)	1.013-1.043 (1.028)
Watermelon	9	1.040

From the Author

Greetings fellow distillers. Just a short bio about my background. I grew up in the hills of North Clark County in Washington State. I earned a Bachelor of Science Degree in Agriculture and a Bachelor of Arts Degree in Economics from Washington State University, Pullman, WA. I also have a Masters Degree in Technical Education from City University, Seattle, WA. After college I taught High School Agriculture Science, Agribusiness, Animal Science, Agricultural Biology and Horticulture for 32 years. I learned the distilling process at a licensed craft distillery in Washington State and have over 10 years of successful distilling experience. I have conducted countless hours of my own distilling research in my quest to perfect the home distilling process. As a technical educator I developed the ability to write instructional materials that are clear, concise, and affective in meeting the goal of teaching people how to do things; in this case, creating top-shelf spirits. I currently live with my wife Sandra in Cowlitz County, Washington State, a rural county where the art of distilling is highly appreciated.

Made in the USA
Las Vegas, NV
04 December 2023

82122479R00090